Communication: Graphic Arts

Modular Exploration of Technology Series

Communication: Graphic Arts

Darvey E. Carlsen

Professor Emeritus
State University College
Oswego, New York

Vernon A. Tryon

State University College
Oswego, New York

Consulting Editor
Rex Miller

PRENTICE-HALL, INC., Englewood Cliffs, New Jersey

Library of Congress Cataloging in Publication Data

Carlsen, Darvey E
   Communication—graphic arts.

   (Modular exploration of technology series)
   Bibliography: p.
   Includes index.
   SUMMARY: Includes such information as major printing
processes, measurement, graphic arts materials and
techniques, planning for reproduction and production,
and finishing operations.
   1. Printing, Practical—Juvenile literature.
(1. Printing, Practical)   I. Tryon, Vernon A.,
1936-   joint author.   II. Title.
Z244.C267   686.2′2   75-12635
ISBN 0-13-153197-2
ISBN 0-13-153189-1 pbk.

MODULAR EXPLORATION OF TECHNOLOGY SERIES

Communication: Graphic Arts

Darvey E. Carlsen, Vernon A. Tryon

10 9 8 7 6 5

PRENTICE-HALL INTERNATIONAL, INC., London
PRENTICE-HALL OF AUSTRALIA, PTY. LTD., Sydney
PRENTICE-HALL OF CANADA, LTD., Toronto
PRENTICE-HALL OF INDIA PRIVATE LTD., New Delhi
PRENTICE-HALL OF JAPAN, INC., Tokyo

Modular Exploration of Technology Series

This book is one module in the MODULAR EXPLORATION OF TECHNOLOGY SERIES. *Modular* means that each topic is presented in a separate book. Modularization produces compact, low-cost text and reference materials to suit any need and any course-organizational pattern. The flexibility afforded by modularization permits schools to select program components best suited to needs and time available.

Exploration means that the world is opened up for investigation. The MET Series is not merely a group of "how-to" books. It does explain how to work with wood, fix engines, and make electronic devices. But exploration implies more than that. The MET Series opens to readers the creative spirit of men and women, the excitement of discovery, and the rewards of patient research. MET readers will study many and various technologies. At the same time, creative "hands-on" activities will reduce abstractions and increase motivation.

Preface

COMMUNICATION: GRAPHIC ARTS provides a basic understanding of graphic arts as a means of communication. Planning procedures, the materials used, and various printing processes are discussed in detail. There are activities for you to work on to help you gain practical experience in graphic arts.

Contents

This unit will acquaint you with the four major printing processes. The graphic arts industry is concerned with the reproduction of images made up of words, symbols, photographs, and illustrations to communicate a message.

1. **You will be able to identify each of the four printing processes commonly used in industry today.**

2. **You will be able to appropriately select a printing process suitable for the material you wish to reproduce.**

3. **You will be able to point out the advantages and disadvantages of each major printing process.**

RELIEF (LETTERPRESS)

Letterpress (relief) is a printing process that has been widely used since the invention of movable type by Johann Gutenberg over 500 years ago. In this printing process, the image to be printed is on a raised (relief) surface. The nonprinting area is lower than the printing area. The image area is inked and a piece of paper is then placed over the inked image. With pressure the ink is transferred from the relief surface to the paper. See Figure 1–1.

Both large and small printing plants still use the relief printing process. Large-circulation publications as well as many small printing plants use the relief process for much of their work. Letterheads, business cards, announcements, and work of that type are frequently reproduced by the relief

FIGURE 1–1
Relief printing.

process. Until very recently almost all type was cast from hot metal.

For hand composition, each individual letter, or *character,* is cast and placed in a storage drawer called a type case. The person who assembles the characters is called a *hand compositor.* For a larger volume of work, the linotype machine (or similar machines) are used to assemble type molds called *matrixes* (molds) of the characters. Matrixes are assembled into lines that are cast in hot metal, forming a line of type on a metal base called a slug. After the type has been composed, it is assembled into forms. Sometimes these are used to print directly on the paper.

Industry is changing the method of assembling images to be reproduced. Type is being composed photographically with the aid of computers. From the printout of the photo composing machine, the images for a page or sheet to be photographed and printed are assembled and attached to a backing sheet. From this *paste-up,* relief plates, called photoengravings, are made by etching the image on a metal or plastic plate. The page to be reproduced is photographed to produce a negative. The negative is then placed over a piece of plastic or metal that has been sensitized. This is then exposed to a strong light, which hardens the light-sensitive *emulsion* (coating) on the plate that is exposed. Light passing through the image area of the negative hardens the emulsion on the plate. The plate is then placed in an *etcher.* For metal plates the material used to etch is an acid. The hardened emulsion on the plate resists the acid and the nonimage area is etched in the plate. This leaves the image area raised above the nonimage area. In some cases the printing will be done directly from the plate. In other instances another plate will be made by forming a matrix mold of the plate from which a *stereotype* (a metal cast) is then made. Rubber printing plates, which are used for printing on metal and many plastic materials are also made from a matrix.

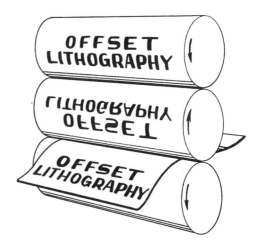

FIGURE 1–2
Offset lithography.

PLANOGRAPHIC (OFFSET LITHOGRAPHY)

Aloys Senefelder developed the lithographic principle in 1798. *Offset lithography,* a planographic printing process, is based on the principle that water and grease will not mix. It is called *planography* because the plate used for printing is on a level plane. This means that the image to be printed is neither raised above the surface nor engraved below the surface. See Figure 1–2. The image to be printed is photographically transferred to the lithographic plate. The plate is made in such a way that the nonimage area is receptive to moisture. This means that if the surface is moistened, the nonimage area will become wet. The image area repels moisture (it will not become wet), but is receptive to ink. The plate is moistened, then inked; the image area picks up the ink while the nonimage area, which is moist with water, repels the ink. It is possible to print on paper directly from the lithographic plate. However, in most cases, the lithographic plate prints on a rubber blanket, which is a rubber sheet stretched tightly around the blanket cylinder; from the rubber blanket the printed image is transferred to the paper. This is called *offset printing* because the image is transferred from the plate to the rubber blanket and from the blanket it is offset onto the paper. The term *offset* is frequently used to describe this printing process. This process is rapidly replacing printing from relief plates. It is widely used in industry to reproduce almost all kinds of printed material. There is little printed material that is reproduced from relief plates that cannot be reproduced with a planographic process.

Offset lithography has several advantages over the relief process. Lithographic plates cost considerably less than relief plates to print the same job. Presses required to print by the offset process are considerably lighter in construction than similar relief presses. Another advantage of this process is that the image is transferred from a plate to a blanket that is soft and resilient. This makes it easier to print on rough surfaces.

SCREEN PRINTING

Screen printing has been used for centuries to reproduce printed material. It is a form of stencil printing; the screen is used to adhere to a *stencil,* which outlines the design. The design itself is open in the sten-

cil. The nondesign area or nonimage area is closed. This printing process is frequently referred to as *silk screen printing.* See Figure 1–3. Silk is frequently used as the fabric, or screen, which holds the stencil during printing. However, in recent years other fabrics have been introduced, such as nylon and stainless steel.

Not only is screen printing an important industrial printing process, but it is also a popular leisure-time activity. Very good reproduction can be made with very inexpensive equipment. In most graphic arts laboratories, screen printing is usually available. In industry, very elaborate presses have been made to automate the process of reproduction.

In this process a stencil is made of the design. The simplest stencil might be a piece of paper with a circle or a rectangle cut out of it. Another stencil material that is sometimes used is a *gelatinous* ma-

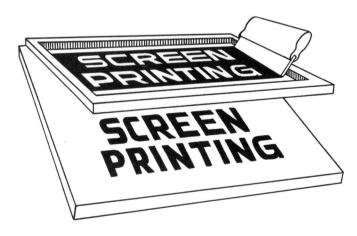

FIGURE 1–3
Screen printing.

terial (like jelly) on a wax or plastic base. The design is placed under the transparent stencil material and with a sharp knife the gelatinous material is cut and peeled away from the image area, while the nonimage part is held on the wax or plastic base. The stencil is then attached to the screen. Stencils are also made photographically. An opaque design can be drawn on a transparent material such as acetate to make a transparent positive. In other words, a transparent positive is any opaque image on a transparent base. Designs may also be made on nontransparent material such as paper. In this case, the transparent positive is made photographically.

Photographic stencil material is a light-sensitive emulsion on a transparent acetate base. The transparent positive is placed in close contact with the stencil material and exposed to light. The light hardens the emulsion in the nonimage area. When the stencil is developed and washed the gelatin in the image area is washed away and in the nonimage area it remains on the acetate. The stencil is then attached to the screen. In the image area the screen is open and in the nonimage area the screen is closed, producing a stencil.

INTAGLIO (GRAVURE)

Intaglio printing (gravure) is a very important printing process al-though not commonly known to most people. The *gravure plate* is made with the image etched below the surface of the plate. The plate is inked with a very thin ink which is retained by wells in the image area (*wells*), and the nonimage area is removed with a scraper called a *doctor blade.* The paper is then impressed against the plate and pulls the ink from the wells etched below the surface of the plate. Almost all authorities agree that gravure is one of the best ways of reproducing fine detail, particularly in photographs, and is especially adaptable to very long runs. By *long runs* we mean over 100,000 copies of the same thing. Intaglio printing is widely used to print food wrappers such as for candy bars. It is also used in long-run publications for mass distribution where many photographs are used. It is not the best method for reproducing reading material such as textbooks or novels. In the graphic arts laboratory it is primarily used as a fine arts medium rather than a production medium. In the fine arts we are concerned primarily with a *limited run* (number of copies printed) that we can use for display purposes. As a practical matter, a production run with this process is next to impossible in the average graphic arts laboratory. Therefore, activities with the *intaglio* process (in other words, where the image is below the surface) are usually limited to scribing the design to be reproduced in a piece of plastic.

To make a reproduction, the design is inked, the nonimage area is wiped clean, and paper is pressed against the plate. It is also common practice to use a piece of metal for making the plate. An *acid resist* (a substance that resists acid) is placed over the whole surface and the image is then scribed in the acid resist. This is placed in an acid bath and the lines that have been scribed through the acid resist are then etched below the surface. See Figure 1–4. The printing procedure is the same as for a plastic plate and the resulting print is commonly referred to as an *etching.* Most plants and industries that utilize the intaglio process for the reproduction of printed material are highly specialized, and frequently it is the only type of reproduction done by the particular plant. In this book very little emphasis is placed upon the intaglio printing process, commonly referred to as *gravure printing* in industry.

We have described four different methods of reproduction. This does not mean that these are the only ways that an image can be reproduced in multiple copies. Other methods of reproduction include ditto (that is, spirit duplication), mimeograph, Xerox, or other photographic means of reproducing copies. However, none of these are considered industrial printing processes. Therefore, this book will discuss only those methods of reproduction that are commonly used by the printing industry.

It is often possible to reproduce an image by any one of the four

FIGURE 1–4
Intaglio printing.

methods that have been described, although in some instances it is better to use one method than another method. For example, in many cases it would be possible to reproduce the same image (the same design) by either *letterpress*, which is relief printing; by *planographic printing*, which is offset lithography; or by *screen printing*.

This book will show you when you might select one process rather than another. It will help you to understand how a reproduction is made by each process. But not in every case will it reflect the most common practice as far as industry is concerned. In many cases the facilities available in the graphic arts laboratory will dictate the process that will be used. For example, it may be more practical on a production basis in industry to reproduce a poster by offset, but it might be more practical and less expensive to reproduce the poster by the screen printing process in the graphic arts laboratory.

ACTIVITIES

1. Build Your Vocabulary:
   a. matrixes
   b. emulsion
   c. etcher
   d. offset lithography
   e. silk screen printing
   f. intaglio
2. Find examples of material printed by each of the four major printing processes.
3. Select three items you would like to reproduce and indicate the printing process you believe would be most appropriate for reproduction.

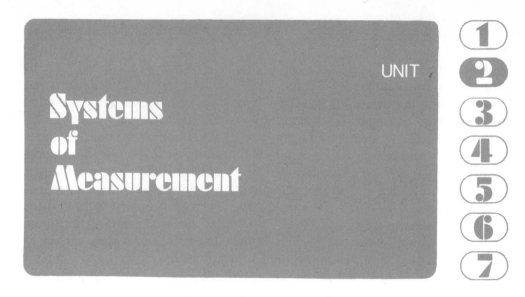

Systems of Measurement

This unit will acquaint you with three systems of measurement: (1) U.S. standard, (2) printers' system, and (3) metric system.

1. **You will be able to apply the U.S. standard of measurement in terms of the inch and fractional parts of an inch and the U.S. standard of weight in terms of ounces and pounds to problems in graphic arts.**

2. **You will be able to convert the U.S. standard inch to units of measurement used in the graphic arts industry.**

3. **You will be able to describe the metric system.**

U.S. STANDARD OF WEIGHTS AND MEASURE

In the graphic arts industry the *inch* and fractions of an inch are used to designate paper sizes. The *foot* (12 inches), the *yard* (36 inches), and the *mile* (5,280 feet) are not commonly used in this field. The terms *pound* and *ounce* are frequently used. The weight of paper is designated in *pounds*. In mixing solutions used to develop film and photographic stencils the fluid *ounce* is the most common unit of measurement. There are 32 fluid ounces in one quart.

The *printers' system* of measurement is universally used to indicate sizes of type and many other measurements in graphic arts. The system was devised so that in referring to small sizes it would *not* be necessary to think and work in terms of fractions of an inch. The system is simple. Its two basic terms are the *pica* and the *point.* There are 6 picas in one inch and 12 points in one pica. Therefore, there are 72 points in one inch. It follows then that 12 point type is 1/6 inch in height and 36 point type is 1/2 inch in height. See Figure 2–1. The *line gauge* is a measuring instru- ment used by printers; it looks somewhat like an ordinary ruler. See Figure 2–2. Note that "inches" are indicated on one edge and the printers' point system on the other.

The printers' system of mea- surement makes it easier to work with small units because it does not

12 Point Type

FIGURE 2–1
Type sizes in points.

36 Point Type

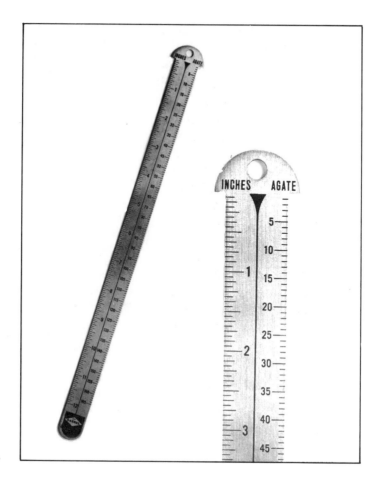

FIGURE 2–2
Typical line gauge.

require the use of fractional parts of an inch to indicate the width of a line of type or the height of a type character. For example, the width of a line of type of 2 ½ inches is expressed as 15 picas; the size of type 14/72 of an inch is expressed as 14 point type; spacing between lines of type 1/24 of an inch is expressed as 3 points.

In the *metric system* there are three basic units: (1) *meter:* a little longer than a yard (about 1.1 yards); (2) *liter:* a little larger than a quart (about 1.6 quarts); and (3) *gram* (about the weight of a paper clip). There are also three common prefixes used with the basic units. (The *prefix,* placed before the term, describes the unit of measure.) They are: milli, which means 1/1,000 (0.001); centi, which means 1/100 (0.01); and kilo, which means 1,000 times (1,000). For example, one millimeter (0.001) is 1/1,000 of a meter. One centimeter (0.01) is 1/100 of a meter. One kilometer is 1,000 meters. One kilogram is equal to 1,000 grams, and one millimeter is equal to (0.001) 1/1,000 of a liter.

Temperature in the metric system is expressed in degrees Celsius, more commonly referred to as degrees centigrade. Water freezes at 0° centigrade and water boils at 100° centigrade.

Adoption of the metric system of weights and measurements by the graphic arts industry would make it possible to eliminate the point system. This would be practi-

cal because small measurements are easier to define and understand using the metric system. However, because at this time the metric system of measurement has not been adopted, and because its use is limited in the graphic arts industry, it will not be used in this book.

Tables 2–1 to 2–3 provide additional illustrations of the metric

TABLE 2-1 MEASUREMENT—LINEAR

1 kilometer (km) = 1,000 meters
1 hectometer (hm) = 100 meters
1 decameter (dkm) = 10 meters
1 decimeter (dm) = 0.1 meter
1 centimeter (cm) = 0.01 meter
1 millimeter (mm) = 0.001 meter
1 micron (u) = 0.000001 meter
= 0.001 millimeter
1 millimicron (mu) = 0.000000001 meter
= 0.001 micron = 0.0000001 millimeter
1 angstrom (A) = .0001 micron
= .1 millicron

TABLE 2-2 VOLUME

1 hectoliter (hl) = 100 liters
1 decaliter (dkl) = 10 liters
1 deciliter (dl) = 0.1 liter
1 centiliter (cl) = 0.01 liter
1 milliliter (ml) = 0.001 liter
= 1.000028 cubic centimeters

TABLE 2-3 WEIGHT

1 metric ton (t) = 1,000 kilograms
1 hectogram (hg) = 100 grams
1 decagram (dkg) = 10 grams
1 decigram (dg) = 0.1 gram
1 centigram (ch) = 0.01 gram
1 milligram (mg) = 0.001 gram

system in relation to measurement, volume, and weight. These examples of measurement, volume, and weight in the metric system were published by the U.S. Department of Commerce, National Bureau of Standards, in Publication No. 233. The abbreviations for each term are indicated in parentheses: for example, 1 kilometer (km). KM is the abbreviation for kilometer.

There are published tables for converting (changing) U.S. standard measurements to the metric system. It would not be difficult to convert the printers' system of measurement to the metric system. However, if the metric system were adopted by the graphic arts industry, the point system would not be necessary and probably would not be used.

ACTIVITIES

1. Build Your Vocabulary:
   a. pica
   b. point
   c. line gauge
   d. metric system
   e. meter
   f. liter
   g. gram

2. Make a plan for reproduction of an image on paper, indicating the size of the paper in inches and the size of the image area in picas.

3. Select a page of this book and record on paper the size of the page in inches and the size of the image area on the page.

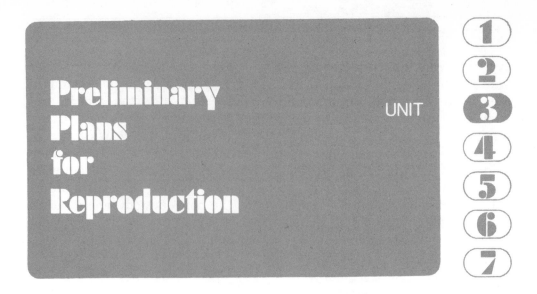

Preliminary Plans for Reproduction

UNIT

1 2 3 4 5 6 7

This unit will acquaint you with accepted practices in the preparation of copy for reproduction and type selection.

1. **You will be able to write simple copy for reproduction.**
2. **You will be able to prepare copy for reproduction.**
3. **You will be able to calculate percentages of enlargement or reduction.**
4. **You will be able to crop photographs.**
5. **You will be able to classify type designs into eight groups.**

WRITING COPY

The key to effective communication begins with writing the *copy*. There are several techniques frequently employed in developing copy. Perhaps the most effective way is to ask the question "What do I wish to communicate?" An example may be the preparation of copy for a business card for a car sales representative. Factors to consider might include (1) make of automobile, (2) dealer's name, (3) dealer's address, (4) name of sales representative, (5) address of sales representative, (6) dealer's telephone, (7) sales representative's telephone number. Figures 3–1 and 3–2 illustrate different treatments of essentially the same copy. Note that in Figure 3–1 the name of the dealer stands out, while in Figure 3–2 the name of the sales representative is most prominent.

After the copy has been written and analyzed the typographer can intelligently proceed to make a layout that will communicate the message in a pleasing manner.

COPY PREPARATION

In graphic arts the term *copy* includes all images to be reproduced.

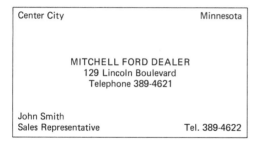

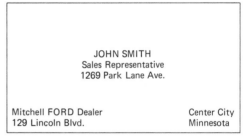

FIGURE 3–1
Dealer's name stands out.

FIGURE 3–2
Salesperson's name stands out.

This includes words, photographs, illustrations, borders, and other ornamentation.

Words, phrases, sentences, and paragraphs should be typewritten with a black ribbon on standard size (8½ X 11) white bond paper substance 20. Double space for normal space between lines, leaving larger spaces between lines where more than normal space is desired in the reproduction. Leave generous margins such as 1½ inches at the top and bottom and 1¼ inches on each side of the page. See Figure 3–3. Clearly number each page in sequence. Avoid word divisions in *manuscripts* (original typewritten copy) prepared for reproduction.

To indicate a continuation of normal space between lines in a manuscript on short pages, draw a vertical line from the last line to the normal bottom margin (Figure 3–4).

When certain copy must be reproduced on a single page, it should be clearly indicated. Even if there are only a few lines, use the entire copy page and in the upper right-hand corner indicate this in paren-

theses. For example, (copy for page 1). See Figure 3–5. Do not include copy for page 2, even if there is room for it on the page. See Figure 3–6.

If two or more pages of copy must be reproduced on a single page, indicate the reproduction page number in the upper right-hand corner, and at the bottom of

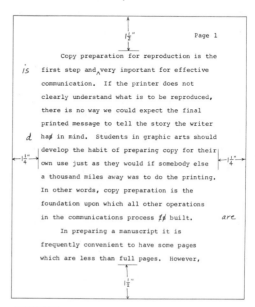

FIGURE 3–3
Margins on copy.

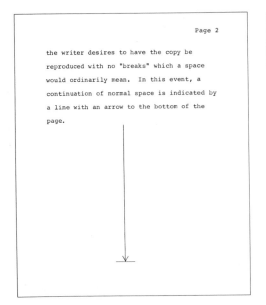

FIGURE 3–4
Continue normal space.

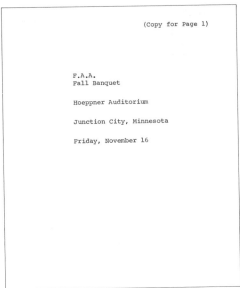

FIGURE 3–5
Copy for single page— RIGHT.

the page typewrite the word "(more)." This will indicate that there is more copy to be included on a given page. See Figure 3–7. At the conclusion of copy for a given page, typewrite "(end of copy for page 2)." See Figure 3–8.

Frequently after a manuscript has been prepared, the author or editor wishes to add words, phrases, or even paragraphs to the original manuscript. If it is only a few words, or a short phrase, this is usually accomplished by inserting it on the page of the original copy. See Figure 3–9. This is one reason for double spacing the typewritten copy. However, more extensive additions are usually made by adding

FIGURE 3–6
Copy for two pages on single sheet—
WRONG.

```
                    (Copy for Page 2)

        If you are preparing copy for a four
    page program and the amount of copy for page
    two is more than one page when typewritten,
    it should be clearly indicated on the copy.
    In the upper right hand corner, indicate the
    page of the program to be printed.
        In a four page program, page one is the
    most visible.  It usually tells three things.
    (1) what, (2) when, and (3) where.  There is
    no firm rule as to order.  Page two is
    considered secondary to page three.  For this
    reason page three is usually reserved for the
    detailed program.  Page two is more appropriate
    for a narrative about the program in general
    or specific information about some aspect of
    the program such as information about the
                        (more)
```

FIGURE 3–7
Indicate more copy for a single page.

```
                    (Copy for Page 2 continued)

    speaker.  When the typographer makes the
    layout for the program he must clearly
    understand that although there are two or
    more pages of typewritten copy he must
    arrange to print it all on page two.


                (End of copy for page 2)
```

FIGURE 3–8
Show end of copy.

one or more pages to the manuscript. When this is necessary, clearly mark the location where the insertion is to be made, such as "Add copy A" for the first addition, "Add copy B" for the second addition, and so on. See Figure 3–10. The page to be added should be numbered the same as the preceding page, followed by the lowercase letter "a" for the first page, "b" for the second page, and so on. See Figure 3–10.

A *cat and rat sign* (or number sign #) may be used to indicate the end of a piece of copy. Newswriters frequently indicate the end of a story with "-30-." This also means the end.

```
                                        Page 4

    v        Word divisions at the ends of lines in
        manuscript copy should be avoided.  This saves
        the compositor (or keyboard operator) time
                                             make
        because it is not necessary for this person to ^
        a decision as to whether or not the word is to
        be hyphenated,
  (add       Word divisions at the ends of lines in
  copy)                                         words
        printed material are frequently used.  When ^
        are hyphenated, the division should always be
        between syllables.  Word divisions of single
        letter syllables such as "a-bout" should be
        avoided.
```

FIGURE 3–9
Mark location of insertion.

```
Copy A                              Page 4a

        Hyphenated words at the ends of printed

  lines are made in order to eliminate unusual

  spacing between words of the line.  In other

  words, they make it easier to maintain an

  even margin on the left and right of the

  printed column.
```

FIGURE 3–10
Identify copy to be added.

PREPARATION OF PHOTOGRAPHS AND ILLUSTRATIONS

Location of Photographs and Illustrations

In the preparation of copy for reproduction it is very important to indicate the location and position of photographs and illustrations. Usually the original manuscript sent to the printer will indicate the ideal location of the photo or illustration, but the exact location will be determined by the person making the final layout. As a general rule, the photo or illustration should be located as close as possible to the text that refers to it. For technical reasons, the ideal placement may not be possible. For example, a one-half page illustration cannot be placed in the bottom one-third of a page. Although this may be the ideal place for it, it must be carried forward to the next page.

ENLARGEMENT AND REDUCTION OF PHOTOGRAPHS AND ILLUSTRATIONS

The most frustrating problem of the layout artist and printer is the customer who submits illustrations or photos that cannot be fitted into the spaces designated in his copy.

Original copy of illustrations or photos can be reduced or enlarged. It should be remembered that enlargements magnify defects; reductions reduce defects. As a rule of thumb, always plan a reduction rather than an enlargement if possible.

The first thing to remember is that reductions (or enlargements) are *proportional.* For example, a photograph that is narrow in width and long in depth will be in these same proportions when it is reduced; a reduction will reduce the width and will also reduce the depth. See Figure 3–11. Conversely, an enlargement will increase the width, but also will increase the depth. See Figure 3–12.

The illustrations in Figures 3–11 and 3–12 both show how the diagonal of a rectangle or square can

FIGURE 3–11
Enlargements are proportional.

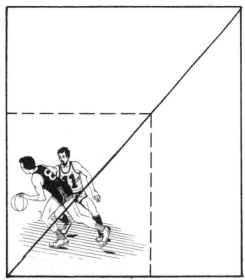

FIGURE 3–12
Reductions are proportional.

be used to visualize the final results of making an enlargement or a reduction. They show that the weight (or strength) of a line is decreased in the reduction and increased in an enlargement. Too frequently consideration is given only to the overall size of the reproduction without consideration of line weight which is of great importance for satisfactory reproduction. In other words, an illustration reduced to 60 per cent of original size will not only be smaller in the reproduction size, but the lines in the illustration will also be thinner. Therefore, a very fine line (*hairline*) in original art work, reduced to 60 per cent of original size, may be so fine that it will be lost in reproduction.

A *proportion scale* is frequently used to calculate enlargements and reductions. See Figure 3–13. To find the percentage of enlargement or reduction, line up present size on Original Size scale (inside scale) under desired new size on Reproduction Size scale (outside scale). Percentage will appear in window. (Some proportion scales work slightly differently.)

For example: Original size is 6 inches, desired reproduction size is 4½ inches. (1) Line up the 6 inch mark on the Original Size scale with the 4½ inch mark on the Reproduction Size scale—circle A. (2) Read the percent of reproduction in the window on the scale; 75 percent —circle B.

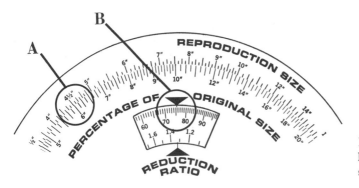

FIGURE 3–13
Reading the reproduction scale.

FIGURE 3–14
Crop marks. (Howard Rose, Jr.)

Cropping Photographs

Almost *never* will an original photograph be the correct size to fit a particular situation. Usually it is necessary to alter width or depth or exclude portions not needed. This is called *cropping.* Creative cropping of photographs provides the typographer an opportunity not only to improve the appearance of the photograph, but also to make the photograph fit the available space. To prepare a photograph for cropping, mount it on a suitable heavy white background. Make the crop marks in the margins (not on the photograph). See Figure 3–14. It is also desirable to attach a transparent tissue over the photograph on which

FIGURE 3–15
Marks on tissue outline the part for reproduction.

lines may be drawn to outline the portion of the photograph to be reproduced. See Figure 3–15.

TYPE SELECTION

After the copy has been written and prepared for reproduction, sizes and styles of type must be selected. From the thousands of designs available, it is bewildering to make selections of type designs without some method of narrowing the field. Effective communication depends upon appropriate type selection.

There are several ways in which all type designs can be classified. Eight major divisions are: (1) oldstyle, (2) transitional, (3) modern, (4) sans serif, (5) square serif, (6) text, (7) cursive, and (8) occasional. Even a limited type library should have type designs in each of these categories.

We have selected classic examples to illustrate each major type classification. It is important to keep in mind that some designs meet every criterion set forth and do not perfectly fit into a particular classification. However, a classification of types is useful, even though not everyone would classify all type designs the same, any more than two people would sort works of art in exactly the same way.

Terms used to describe the various elements (parts) of a type face are illustrated in Figure 3–16.

Examples of Major Type Designs

Oldstyle. We have selected Caslon to point out the identifying characteristics of oldstyle type. In Figure 3–17 you will note a moderate variation in thickness of the letters; serifs are bracketed, and irregular; lower-

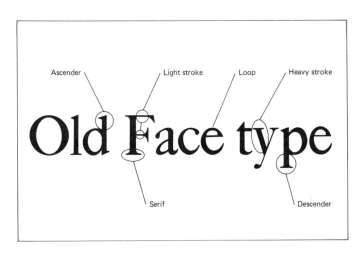

FIGURE 3–16
Type face terms.

ABCDEFGHIJKLMN
QRSTUVW

abcdefghijklmnopqrstuvw

FIGURE 3–17
Caslon Old Style.

case *t* does not have a distinct cross; serifs on the uppercase *T* are angular, not straight; loops and counters are relatively small; ascenders (such as *b,d,h*) and descenders(such as *g, j, p*) are about medium length.

Modern. In comparison with oldstyle, modern type designs have a greater variation in thickness of stroke; serifs are not bracketed, and are uniform and regular; the cross stroke on the lowercase *t* is straight and precise; serifs on the uppercase *T* are straight and uniform; counters and loops are larger; ascenders and descenders are shorter. The letter formation has a mechanical appearance. It is sharper and has more fine detail. In Figure 3–18 note the circled portions that illustrate these characteristics.

Transitional. Transitional type designs such as Baskerville (shown in Figure 3–19) have characteristics of both oldstyle and modern type designs. Transitional type designs historically were made after oldstyle designs, but before modern designs. Oldstyle type was designed for rough textured paper. With the advent of smoother paper, it was possible to reproduce more detail, so it was natural that more fine lines and greater detail were incorporated in transitional type designs.

ABCDEFGHIJKLMNOP
QRST

abcdefghijklmnopqrst

FIGURE 3–19
Baskerville is a transitional type design.

Sans Serif. *Sans* is a French word meaning without. Sans serif type designs have no serifs. Another characteristic is little or no contrast in the thickness of the stroke. It is perhaps the most easily identified type classification we have. Figure

ABCDEFGHIJKLMNOP
QRSTUVW

abcdefghijklmnopqrstuv

FIGURE 3–18
Bodoni is a classic modern type design.

ABCDEFGHIJKLMNOP
QRSTUVWXYZ

abcdefghijklmnopqrstuvw

FIGURE 3–20
Sans serif type designs are easy to identify.

3–20 is a typical example of sans serif type.

Square Serif.   Figure 3–21 shows an example of *Stymie*, which is typical of square serif type designs. Add a square serif to a sans serif type design and the result is a square serif type face.

AFGHIJKLMN

atuvwxyzabcd

FIGURE 3–21
Square serif designs are easy to identify.

Cursive.   Any type design that resembles handwriting can be classified as cursive. This includes a true script, which is an elegant imitation of handwriting, to semiscripts, which are reasonable facsimilies of handwriting. Figure 3–22 shows examples of cursive type.

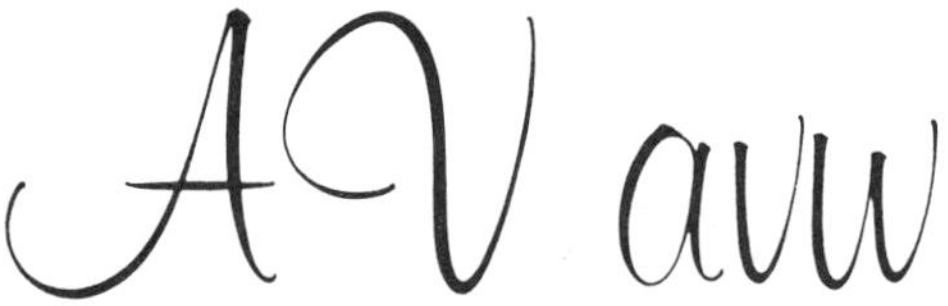

FIGURE 3–22
Cursive types resemble handwriting.

Text.   Text type designs are patterned after the writing of the scribes. It is easy to classify, but difficult to read. Figure 3–23 shows examples of text type.

ABCDEFGH
abcdefghijklmno

FIGURE 3–23
Text type is patterned after writing of scribes.

Occasional.   This classification of type designs groups together all type styles that defy classification. In other words, it is a miscellaneous category into which are placed the designs that are neither "fish nor fowl." If you are completely undecided about a specific classification, identify it as *occasional*. Figure 3–24 shows examples that the authors consider appropriate for this label.

AOPQRSTUV
aopqrstu $789

FIGURE 3–24
Occasional includes designs that defy classification.

Guidelines for Using Major Type Styles

Type styles, like styles of clothing, have periods of popularity and periods when their use is less popular. For example, at the turn of the century, text type was widely used in all types of reproduction, while its use today is limited. Likewise in the twenties Cheltenham, originally designed by Bertram Goodhue, was the rage. In the 1940s and 1950s that design lost popularity. However, in the late 1960s and early 1970s it regained popularity. Likewise in the 1940s and 1950s modern type designs predominated display composition, whereas in the late 1960s and early 1970s oldstyle type design was more commonly used for display lines. Display type is usually 14 point or larger and is used to print headings in books, magazines, and newspapers. Body type is smaller and is used to print reading matter in books, magazines, and newspapers. Typographers and designers reflect the tone of the times. This is not unusual. Most architecture and clothing styles can be identified with periods in our history.

The following very general guidelines are valid for all type styles, regardless of their popularity at any given time. In a discussion of type classification and type styles three terms are frequently encountered.

1. A *family* refers to several variations of a single design. For example, Cheltenham is an oldstyle type design. It is available in many variations, such as Cheltenham Oldstyle, Cheltenham Bold, Cheltenham Bold Condensed, Cheltenham Bold Extra Condensed, Cheltenham Bold Extended, and many others. The Cheltenham family has perhaps more variations than any other oldstyle design. Figure 3–25 gives examples of a few members of the Cheltenham family.

2. A *series* means the sizes available for one member of a type family. For example, in Cheltenham Bold a complete series would include 6 point, 8 point, 10 point, 12 point, 14 point, 18 point, 24 point, 30 point, 36 point, 42 point, 48 point, 54 point, 60 point, 72 point, 84 point, 96 point, and 120 point. See Figure 3–26.

3. A *font* of type is a complete assortment of all characters: upper case, lower case, figures (that is, numbers) punctuation marks, and special characters such as the dollar sign, parenthesis, ampersand, and so on. See Figure 3–27.

Oldstyle. Oldstyle is frequently composed in both upper and lower case, or all upper case. Its use is flexible. Letterspacing (that is, adding thin spacing material between letters) is frequently employed to achieve line length desired. Oldstyle is frequently selected for the composition of text matter (textbooks, novels) and related display lines. For a caption under a picture of "The Old Mill Stream" an oldstyle design would be more appropriate than a modern type design.

Cheltenham Oldstyle
Series Number 87
Designed by Morris F. Benton
Based on design of Bertram Goodhue

Characters in complete font

A B C D E F G H I J K L M N
O P Q R S T U V W X Y Z &
$ 1 2 3 4 5 6 7 8 9 0
a b c d e f g h i j k l m n o p q
r r s t u v w x y z . , - : ; !? ' ' " ( ) [ ] ¶
fi ff fl ffi ffl Qu ct st

Cheltenham Medium
Series Number 83
Designed by Morris F. Benton
Based on design of Bertram Goodhue

Characters in complete font

A B C D E F G H I J K L M N
O P Q R S T U V W X Y Z &
$ 1 2 3 4 5 6 7 8 9 0
a b c d e f g h i j k l m n o p q
r r s t u v w x y z . , - : ; ! ? '
fi ff fl ffi ffl ct st

Cheltenham Bold Extra Condensed
Series Number 70
Designed by Morris F. Benton
Based on design of Bertram Goodhue

Characters in complete font

A B C D E F G H I J K L M N
O P Q R S T U V W X Y Z &
$ 1 2 3 4 5 6 7 8 9 0
a b c d e f g h i j k l m n o p q
r r s t u v w x y z . , - : ; ! ? '
fi ff fl ffi ffl

Cheltenham Bold Extended
Series Number 72
Designed by Morris F. Benton
Based on design of Bertram Goodhue

Characters in complete font

A B C D E F G H I J K L M N
O P Q R S T U V W X Y Z &
$ 1 2 3 4 5 6 7 8 9 0
a b c d e f g h i j k l m n o p q
r r s t u v w x y z . , - : ; ! ? '

Cheltenham Bold
Series Number 67
Designed by Morris F. Benton
Based on design of Bertram Goodhue

Characters in complete font

A B C D E F G H I J K L M N
O P Q R S T U V W X Y Z &
$ 1 2 3 4 5 6 7 8 9 0
a b c d e f g h i j k l m n o p q
r s t u v w x y z . , - : ; ! ? '

Cheltenham Bold Condensed
Series Number 68
Designed by Morris F. Benton
Based on design of Bertram Goodhue

Characters in complete font

A B C D E F G H I J K L M·N
O P Q R S T U V W X Y Z &
$ 1 2 3 4 5 6 7 8 9 0
a b c d e f g h i j k l m n o p q
r r s t u v w x y z . , - : ; ! ? '

Cheltenham Bold Outline
Series Number 75
Characters in complete font

A B C D E F G H I J K
L M N O P Q R S T
U V W X Y Z &
$ 1 2 3 4 5 6 7 8 9 0
a b c d e f g h i j k l m n
o p q r r s t u v w x y z
. , - - : ; ! ? ' '

FIGURE 3–25
Members of Cheltenham family.

Caution should be exercised in mixing oldstyle designs with modern or sans serif designs in the same job. Its use is recommended for, but not limited to, rough textured stock. It does not look well with more than normal space between lines when a paragraph is composed, or when a series of lines appear in a group together. It is not considered the best type style for *reverse prints* where the background of the type is

ABCDEFGHIJKLMNOPQRSTUVWXYZ
8 point Cheltenham Bold

ABCDEFGHIJKLMNOPQR
14 point Cheltenham Bold

ABCDEFGHIJKLMNOPQ
18 point Cheltenham Bold

FIGURE 3-26
Partial series of Cheltenham Bold.

ABCDEFGHIJKLMNO
24 point Cheltenham Bold

printed and the type appears in the color of the stock on which it is printed. See Figure 3–28.

Modern Type. Modern is available in small and large sizes. Most authorities do not consider classic modern type designs to be as easily readable in paragraphs as oldstyle type designs. For this reason they are not frequently used to print novels or textbooks. Modern looks better with more extensive letter-spacing and with greater than normal space between lines than does oldstyle. Modern type is most effective on smooth paper and is most appropriately combined with sans serif, square serif, limited cursive, and occasional type designs. A caption under a picture of modernistic architecture would be more appropriately composed in modern than in oldstyle type. It combines least well with oldstyle and text type designs.

Transitional. Transitional type faces have characteristics of both old-style and modern designs. Baskerville is a classic example. It is most frequently used for text composition in novels and textbooks. This design is also available in both large and small sizes, but is used most frequently in sizes from 9 to 12 point.

Bernhard Modern Roman

Series Number 668
Designed by Lucian Bernhard
Characters in complete font

A B C D E F G H I J K L M N
O P Q R S T U V W X Y Z &
$ 1 2 3 4 5 6 7 8 9 0 ¢
a b c d e f g h i j k l m n o p q
r s t u v w x y z . , - : ; ! ? ' ' " " §

FIGURE 3-27
A font of type.

How to prepare artwork

FIGURE 3–28
A reverse print.

Sans Serif. Sans serif type designs are available from small to large sizes. Their most frequent use is in display composition and in a few lines grouped together in smaller sizes. Most of the sans serif designs have large families, from very light to very bold, and from condensed to extended letters. This design is flexible in spacing, both in letterspace (especially in the bold versions) and in space between lines. It is frequently used in paragraphs and short compositions such as advertisements, sales brochures, and equipment manuals. Most authorities agree that it is not the most legible (easily read) type design for novels or textbooks. Modern, cursive, square serif, and many occasional designs make a pleasing combination with sans serif.

Square Serif. Square serif designs, although not very popular lately, might be characterized as being parallel to sans serif type designs. If there are limitations on a budget for a type library for general use, the authors recommend eliminating square serif designs and expanding upon sans serif designs.

Cursive. Cursive type designs are an imitation of handwriting. Most designs are available from 12 point to the larger sizes (72 point). Very few designs are available in 10 point and none smaller. In comparison with other designs in the major classifications, ascenders and descenders on the letters are long. Therefore the "o," "e," "a," and so on are small in relation to the point size of the type. In small sizes, cursive types have very poor legibility. Cursive types are widely used and are often misused. Almost never should cursive types be set in all uppercase letters because of the many awkward combinations that are hard to read when reproduced. The second most frequent error is to letterspace cursive type. This detracts from the simulation of handwriting and appears unnatural. Two general guidelines are: (1) do not compose cursive type in all uppercase letters, and (2) do not letter-space composition in cursive type. Cursive type is most frequently used in a few words or lines. It is almost never used for text composition. Most frequently only a line or two will be used in a commercial advertisement, a letterhead, business card, title page, or a program cover. "A little goes a long way." An exception to this will be found in formal commercial announcements and personal invitations and announcements such as for weddings, births, and deaths. When minor notations must be made in small sizes of type, a light sans serif is most frequently combined with cursive. Cursive type designs may be used in combination with other major type classifications except text types.

Text. Text type designs were patterned after the writing of the scribes. The guidelines for the use of cursive type may be applied to text type. At the turn of the century, text type was widely used for all types of reproduction. However, its use and application has diminished over the last 75 years. It is still used for special occasions, usually of a religious nature or to imply something old, such as the key line on a business card of an antique dealer.

Occasional. Occasional type designs do not fit any other classifications. They are unusual. In most instances they are 24 point or larger and are used exclusively for display lines. Caution should be given to their use, which should be limited to a few words or to one or two lines. They are usually used as "attention getters" or to more forcefully emphasize tranquility, speed, dignity, strength, or moods of depression or elation. The graphic artist uses occasional type designs to make his work more effective. The beginner more frequently will overuse occasional type, which marks his work as that of an amateur. In other words, occasional is the most difficult type design to use effectively.

Practical Considerations in Type Selection

A typographer (the person making a layout) will seldom be able to use the exact size and style of type he or she believes is ideal. A compromise must be made. For this reason, as a practical matter, we recommend that initial planning and type selection be based upon the classifications and sizes available in the graphic arts laboratory where the work will be done.

ACTIVITIES

1. Building Your Vocabulary:
   - a. copy
   - b. manuscript
   - c. line weight
   - d. cropping
   - e. Cheltenham
   - f. family
   - g. series
   - h. font
2. Write copy for a ticket that might be used for a school activity.
3. Calculate the size of a 4 X 6 photograph reduced to 60 per cent of original size.
4. Find printed examples of each major type design classification.

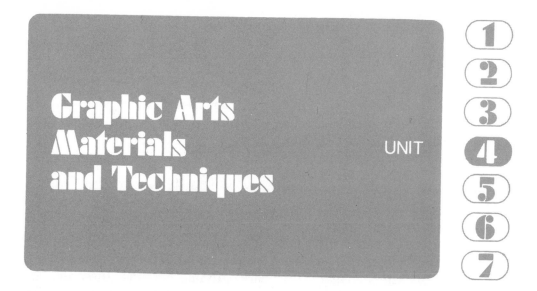

Graphic Arts Materials and Techniques

UNIT

1
2
3
4
5
6
7

This unit will acquaint you with common materials used in image assembly and reproduction to effectively communicate a message.

1. **You will be able to make an appropriate selection of paper with respect to purpose, weight, color, texture, and grain for message reproduction.**

2. **You will be able to estimate the amount of paper required to reproduce a job and to calculate the cost of the paper.**

3. **You will be able to achieve special effects through the use of materials and techniques for more effective communications.**

4. **You will be able to select inks appropriate for relief, offset, and screen printing reproduction.**

5. **You will be able to mix inks to obtain desired color for reproduction.**

PAPER

It is possible to print on almost all surfaces. However, paper is the most common material used in graphic arts for reproduction of printed messages.

You should select the paper for reproduction in the early stages of designing the job. It should be suit- able for the purpose for which it will be used. Daily newspapers are printed on *newsprint.* It is an inexpensive paper that is suitable for large circulation publications that are read today and discarded tomorrow. Permanent records such as birth certificates are printed on high quality rag bond paper that is expensive, but will not change color or fall apart when stored for long periods of time.

Printers buy paper in large sheets or rolls. Some presses are designed to print from rolls but these are seldom found in graphic arts laboratories. Therefore, we will be concerned with paper purchased in sheets.

There are several major kinds or classifications of paper and each one has a basic sheet size. The basic sheet size of any kind of paper is the most efficient size for jobs that are normally printed on that kind of paper. For example, the basic sheet size of bond paper is 17 X 22 inches because bond paper is usually used for letterheads (that is, business writing paper), which are generally 8 ½ X 11 inches.

Printers do not specify the thickness of most papers directly but they do specify the weight, for example 20 pound bond. This means that one ream (500 sheets equal one ream) of 17 X 22 inch bond paper will actually weigh 20 pounds. The substance or basis weight of any paper is the weight in pounds of one ream of the basic sheet size for that kind of paper. In many cases, the larger the substance number the thicker will be the sheets, for example, 20 pound bond (that is, the usual weight of notebook paper) will be thicker than 13 pound bond.

Paper sizes are always designated in inches so it is not necessary to specify inches when referring to paper sizes.

The basic sheet size for the common kinds of paper are:

- Bond, 17 X 22
- Book, 25 X 38
- Cover, 20 X 26
- Index Bristol, 25 ½ X 30 ½

Paper, like wood, has grain because it is made up of fibers. In the paper making process more fibers are aligned in the direction in which the paper moves through the machine. Paper is available with the grain running either in the direction of the short dimension or in the direction of the long dimension of the sheet. In paper catalogs and on paper package labels, grain direction is indicated by underlining the dimension in which the grain runs. For example, book paper labeled 25 X 38 means the grain is parallel to the long dimension. Paper folds easier with the grain than against the grain. This is important to remember, especially if the paper must be folded after it has been printed. Whenever possible, fold with the grain. If 3 X 5 cards are to be placed in a typewriter, the grain should be in the direction of the *platen* (roller against which the keys strike) on the typewriter.

There are exceptions to designating paper by its basis weight rather than thickness. Examples are *blanks* and *boards* which are commonly referred to as cardboard.

Thickness of these is indicated as 4 ply (caliper .018), 6 ply (caliper .024), 8 ply (caliper .030), and 10 ply (caliper .36). The *caliper* is in thousandths of an inch, and the basic sheet size is 22 × 28.

Texture refers to the roughness or smoothness of the paper surface. Bond paper, commonly used for business forms and stationery, is available in several finishes (or textures). This is true for all major kinds of papers. Rough textured paper is most suitable for screen printing or offset lithography. Smooth papers are required to reproduce photographs in relief printing.

Paper is available in a rainbow of colors. For maximum visibility, black on white or black on yellow is recommended. Blue ink on blue paper is less visible. Select a paper color that is appropriate to the purpose of your printed job.

Estimating Amount of Paper Needed

To estimate the amount of paper required to print a job, always start with the size of the piece to be printed. For example, if you print 10,000 letterheads on (8 ½ × 11) bond, find out how many 17 × 22 sheets will be required to print the job. Spoilage for a single color might be 3 per cent, or 300 pieces out of a run of 10,000. Therefore, 10,-300 pieces 8 ½ × 11 would be required to print 10,000 letterheads.

The next step in figuring the amount of paper needed is to find the number of 8 ½ × 11 pieces that can be cut from each 17 × 22 sheet. We always make the cuts in such a way as to get the largest number of pieces from each sheet. Divide the dimensions of the desired pieces into the dimensions of the sheet. If the grain direction is important then the division must be done so the grain direction of both pieces correspond.

If the grain direction is not important then the division should be done in two ways and the best arrangement should be used.

	A	B
Sheet size	17 × 22	17 × 22
Piece size	8 ½ × 11	11 × 8 ½
Number of pieces from each sheet	2 × 2 = 4	1 × 2 = 2

Obviously, method A above is the best.

The diagrams in Figure 4–1 show the relationship of the 8 ½ × 11 pieces to the sheet as figured above.

To find the number of sheets required for a job, divide the number of pieces needed by the number that can be cut from one sheet.

$$\frac{\text{Number of pieces required}}{\text{Number of pieces per sheet}} =$$

Number of sheets required

$$4\overline{)10{,}300} \quad 2{,}575$$

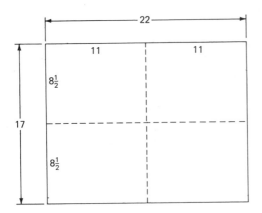
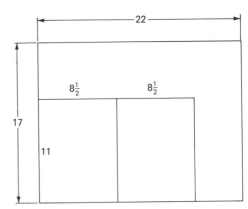

FIGURE 4–1
Diagram pieces per sheet.

You can figure the cost of the paper for a job after you have found the number of sheets of paper required by finding the weight of the paper in pounds. It is easier to calculate the weight of paper on the basis of 1,000 sheets than on the basis of 500 sheets. For this reason, paper catalogs and package labels indicate the weight per thousand sheets. Assume, for this example, we are using substance 20 bond paper. The package would be marked 17 X 22–40M; this means 1000 sheets would weigh 40 pounds (M is the Roman numeral designation for 1,000)

$$\frac{\text{no. of sheets} \times \text{wt. of 1,000 sheets}}{1000}$$

= wt. of paper for the job.
2.575 × 40 = 103 lbs.

To divide by 1,000, move the decimal point three places to the left.
If we further assume the cost per pound is $50 per 100 pounds (50¢ per pound), to find the cost, multiply the number of pounds of paper by the cost per pound;

no. of lbs. of paper × cost per lb.
= cost of paper for the job

103 × $.50 = $51.50 cost of paper

In this example, there is no waste since all of the sheet can be used. Whenever possible, select a sheet size that can be cut without waste.

INK

Three important factors in selection of ink are: (1) printing process, (2) material to be printed, and (3) color.
Printing inks are basically made up of pigment, vehicle, and drier. The *pigment* imparts color, the *vehicle* forms the body of the ink, and the *drier* aids in making

the ink dry on the surface. This is a simplification. Actually ink is a complex chemical mixture. It is scientifically formulated to meet the requirements of a process and be chemically suitable for sticking to and drying on a variety of surfaces.

Inks are available for all processes and for printing on almost all materials. Consult the manufacturers' technical bulletins in selecting the ink most suitable for a particular purpose and process.

Most graphic arts laboratories stock inks suitable for printing on paper. In addition, we will describe some special inks for fabrics and plastics. It is not possible to stock all colors, and therefore it is frequently necessary to mix inks to obtain a specific color. From the three primary colors, which are red, yellow, and blue, plus white and black, it is possible to mix any other colors. A combination of yellow and blue produces green; yellow and red produce orange; and red and blue produce purple. Use a color wheel as a guide in mixing ink. It is important that the dark color be added to the light color when mixing ink. It takes a very small amount of blue added to yellow to produce green. You should mix a little more ink than you think you will need for a particular job.

Color selection of both paper and ink is often based on personal choice. Sometimes that is acceptable and the finished job looks pleasing. However, because colors have the ability to convey a mood, the person selecting paper or ink for a job must choose a color that is appropriate for the job. Research has demonstrated that certain colors suggest certain feelings, seasons, or ideas. For example, red can be associated with heat, St. Valentines Day, or rage.

Here is a brief list of some colors and what various psychologists have found them to mean. *Red*—brilliant, hot, fire, Christmas, danger, Fourth of July, excitement, fierceness, activity, intensity. *Orange*—bright, glowing, warm, autumnal, Halloween, jovial, lively, forceful, hilarity. *Yellow*—sunny, radiant, sunlight, caution, cheerful, inspiring, vital, Godly, health, high spirits. *Green*—clear, moist, cool, nature, water, quieting, St. Patrick's Day, refreshing, peaceful, terror, guilt. *Blue*—wet, transparent, cold, sky, ice, service, sober, melancholy, gloom, fearful, flag. *Purple*—deep, soft, atmospheric, cool, mist, dark, shadow, Easter, mourning, dignified, pompous, regal, loneliness, desperation. *White* —light, space, cool, snow, clean, Mother's Day, pure, frank, youthful, normality, brightness of spirit. *Black*—darkness, space, night, neutral, emptiness, funeral, ominous, deadly, depression, negation of spirit.*

*Alling and Cory, *Printing Salesman's Newsletter.*

SPECIAL EFFECTS

There is a wide variety of materials available to attain special effects in jobs to be reproduced. All are easy to use but many require experimentation and practice to develop the most pleasing results. Special effects are most practical in the areas of screen printing and offset lithography. In each instance, it is possible to make the same reproduction with relief printing. However, the equipment and skills required to make relief plates are more complex. For this reason their application in graphic arts laboratories is limited.

Zip-a-Tone

Zip-a-Tone is available in a variety of patterns and designs. See Figure 4–2. The design is printed on adhesive-backed transparent material mounted on a paper base. Place a piece of Zip-a-Tone over the design, and with a sharp knife cut and peel away the nonprinting area.

The example of a student handbook cover illustrates the use of Zip-a-Tone in the design. See Figure 4–3. The outer lines of the rectangle show the paper size on which the cover design is to be printed. Note that this is larger than the finished size, which is indicated by lines of

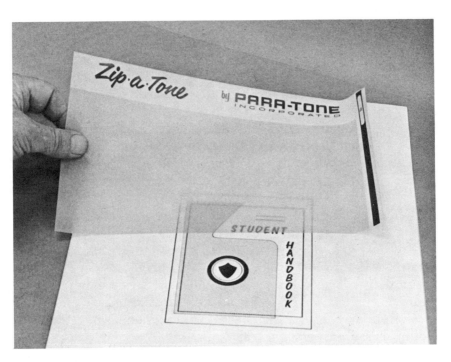

FIGURE 4–2
Zip-a-Tone for background designs.

FIGURE 4–3
Student handbook cover.

quired on the *gripper edge* (*grippers* are devices to hold the sheet in the press while being printed) in which no image can be reproduced. For most presses, a minimum of ¼ inch is required for gripper bite on the gripper edge. In this example, the gripper edge was at the top. Also, nonprinting space is frequently required on each side to provide space for *ejection* rollers, which deliver the sheet after it has been printed. On presses that require ejection rolls for delivery, a minimum of ½ inch of nonprinting area is recommended on each side of the sheet. A small space is recommended for the fourth side (bottom in this example) so the entire image is printed on the sheet. About 1/16 inch is considered a minimum.

Reverse Prints and Surprints

Reverse prints and surprints, combined with screen tints and photographs, provide many opportunities for creative application of special effects. See Figure 4–4. In a *reverse print,* the image area becomes the color of the paper. *Surprinting* is printing a solid image over a lighter background. In Figure 4–4 the image is lines of type. An examination of the example shows that a reverse print is most effective with a dark background, and a surprint is most effective with a light background.

Screen tint backgrounds may be prepared using Zip-a-Tone, as illus-

the smaller rectangle. In other words, the finished cover will be trimmed after being printed to the size indicated by the inside rectangle.

This also illustrates two important factors that must be taken into consideration in making plans for reproduction. First, the tinted area background in this example is a *bleed.* That means the printed image runs over the outer edges. Whenever a bleed is printed, it should extend beyond the trim line. Second, the size of the paper on which the image is printed must be larger than the finished size. This is necessary because blank space is re-

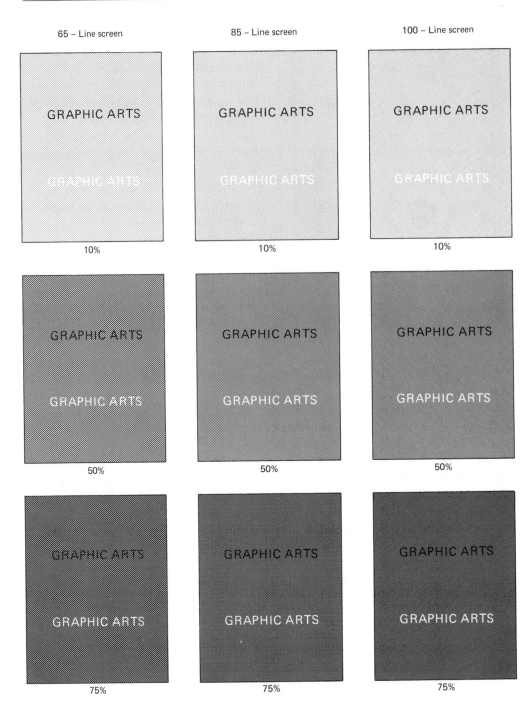

FIGURE 4–4
Examples of surprint and reverse print on typical screen tint background.

trated in Figure 4–2. Screen tints may also be made by inserting a screen between a negative or positive and the plate. A positive is the opposite of a negative. The image on a positive is opaque on a transparent background while on a negative the image is transparent on an opaque background. In making a printing plate, or a screen stencil requiring a screen tint, the screen is placed between the negative or positive and the plate or stencil film before exposure.

Screen tints are available from coarse to fine. A coarse screen has 65 lines per inch, and a fine screen has 100 lines per inch. The *density* (that is, darkness) of the screen is designated in percentage of area covered by opaque dots. For example, a light tint might be 10 per cent and a dark tint (almost solid) 90 per cent. For offset lithography, fine screens (100 line) or coarse screens (65 line) will make good reproductions. However, for screen printing, only the coarse screen is recommended.

Surprints are frequently combined with halftones to achieve special effects. Figure 4–5 illustrates the results of this procedure.

The procedure used to reproduce Figure 4–5 was as follows.

1. A charcoal drawing was produced and a halftone negative was made from the drawing. See (Figure 4–6).

A halftone negative was necessary because the drawing had *tonal value,* that is, shades of gray ranging from white to black. In order to reproduce the tonal values, the original had to be photographed through a halftone screen which produced a series of dots of varying sizes on the negative. In the light, colored areas of the drawing, that is, the highlights, more light was reflected to the film and thus the dots were large in the negative. The opposite was true in the dark colored areas of the drawing, that is, shadows. In the shadow areas, less light was reflected to the film and the dots were smaller. That produced tonal values in the negative that were the reverse of the tonal values in the original drawing. When the printing plate was exposed through the halftone negative, the highlight areas received little exposure light and thus developed a small, open dot pattern on the plate. The shadow areas received more light and developed large dots on the plate. The small dots transmitted relatively little ink; the large dots transmitted much ink; and there was a range of tones corresponding to the tonal range of the original drawing.

2. The type, that is, line copy, to be surprinted over the drawing was composed, *pasted up* in proper position, and photographed to produce a line negative. See Figure 4–7.

3. The halftone negative was stripped into a masking sheet *flat* in the proper position for exposing the plate.

4. The line negative was stripped into a second flat. It was

FIGURE 4–5
Surprint in combination with halftone.

FIGURE 4–6
Halftone of charcoal drawing.

positioned so when the two flats were placed together the type was in the proper location in relation to the drawing. That proper positioning is called *register.*

5. The flat of the halftone negative was placed over the plate and the exposure was made. The flat for the line copy was placed over the same plate and a second exposure was made. See Figure 4–7. The plate was then developed and was ready for the press.

Masking Film

Masking films are another way of producing special effects. Ulano®

Rubylith® is a red "light-safe" stripping film coated on a polyester backing sheet. A special adhesive permits stripped portions to be replaced on the polyester for corrections. The red film can also be transferred to film negatives or positives. Because it is light-safe, the Rubylith attached to a negative or positive will serve the same purpose as the black opaque emulsion of a negative. Rubylith film photographs as if it were black. Amberlith® is similar to Rubylith except it is amber in color, and provides better *see-through.* However, it is not quite as *light-safe* for making lithographic offset plates. It also photographs as black.

GRAPHIC

ARTS

GENERAL PRINTING
MFG. - COM. 160
OSWEGO STATE

Becky L. Allen

FIGURE 4–7
Line copy paste-up.

FIGURE 4–8
Attach film over design. (Ulano Graphic Arts
Supplies, Inc.)

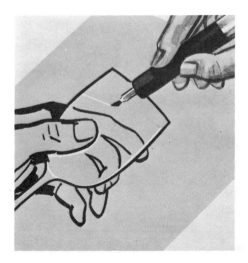

FIGURE 4–9
Cut film with sharp knife. (Ulano Graphic
Arts Supplies, Inc.)

The following procedure is recommended in using masking films. Place the film over the design and attach with tape. With a sharp knife, cut the film and peel away the unwanted film. See Figures 4–8 to 4–11.

Other examples that show the use of Ulano® masking films are shown in Figures 4–12 to 4–16. These illustrations were provided through the courtesy of Ulano Graphic Arts Supplies, 210 East 86th St., New York, New York, 10028.

In Figure 4–12, the background density was reduced by peeling away the film in the dark (shadow) areas and leaving the film in the light (highlight) areas.

The outline of the girl in Figure 4–13 was made by peeling away the film, leaving an opening (window) in the film for just the portion to be printed.

FIGURE 4–10
Peel film from backing sheet. (Ulano Graphic
Arts Supplies, Inc.)

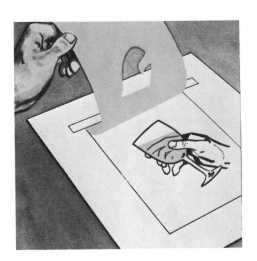

FIGURE 4–11
Window peeled from backing sheet. (Ulano Graphic Arts Supplies, Inc.)

FIGURE 4–12
Reduce background density. (Ulano Graphic Arts Supplies, Inc.)

Although the illustrations here are all in one color, masking films are frequently used to make manual color separations. For example, in Figure 4–14, the parallel lines at the top and sides of the photograph could be printed in a color such as red to enhance the photograph.

Wash art is a method used in water color painting in which a portion of the image is washed out with a damp brush while the painting is still damp. This effect can be attained by using the masking film to block out areas in the image which would otherwise print. See Figure 4–15.

Masking film is convenient for making windows in art work that has a combination of line work (solid lines such as type) and halftones (photographs that have a dot

structure). This is necessary because two separate negatives must be made: one for line work, and one

FIGURE 4–13
Outline halftone negatives. (Ulano Graphic Arts Supplies, Inc.)

FIGURE 4–14
Accurately rule lines. (Ulano Graphic Arts Supplies, Inc.)

FIGURE 4–16
Prepare knockouts or island dropouts. (Ulano Graphic Arts Supplies, Inc.)

FIGURE 4–15
Get wash art from line art. (Ulano Graphic Arts Supplies, Inc.)

for halftones. A line negative is made with masking film stripped in the copy paste-up where a photo-

graph will appear. A halftone negative is then made of the photograph. If space permits, the halftone negative is attached to the underside of the line negative in the window opening produced by the masking film. If the photograph must print within ¼ inch of the line work, it is best that a double exposure be made on the plate: first expose the line work with the windows masked over. Then, for the second exposure, mask out the line work, open the windows, and attach the halftone negative through the window.

Figure 4–16 illustrates a *knockout* or *island dropout.* The portion to be dropped out is cut in the film. The most frequent application of this procedure is in combination with photographs or screen tints.

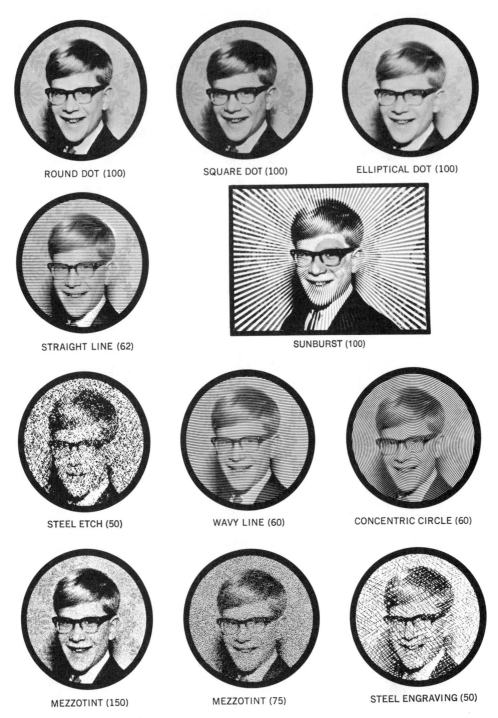

FIGURE 4–17
Special effects with Caprock ® halftones contact screens. (Caprock Developments, Inc.)

Special Effect Halftone Contact Screens

Photographs have tonal value. This means there is a range of tone from light (white) to dark (black). In order to reproduce all of the intermediate tones, a *halftone* negative must be made.

The most common method of making a halftone negative is to use a *halftone contact screen.* The halftone screen is a thin piece of plastic on which is reproduced opaque dots or lines. Figure 4–17 is reproduced through the courtesy of Caprock Developments, Inc., Morris Plains, New Jersey. It illustrates the con-

ventional round dot and square dot screens as well as special effect screens for halftone reproduction.

Posterization

Posterization is frequently used to produce unusual and pleasing effects in the reproduction of photographs. Different tones of the photograph are reproduced as solid line negatives. Figure 4–18 is an example of a photograph reproduced by using conventional halftone techniques.

Posterization of the photograph in Figure 4–19 was accomplished by

FIGURE 4–18
Conventional halftone. (Howard Rose, Jr.)

FIGURE 4–19
Posterization of photograph in Figure 4-18. (Howard Rose, Jr.)

making a line negative (all solid lines, no halftone screen) by increasing the exposure about three times the normal time of a line exposure. For example, if the normal exposure time for a line negative is 15 seconds at f-16, increase the exposure time to 45 seconds at f-16. Note that in Figure 4–19 the resulting print appears as a silhouette that resembles a profile drawing with the outline filled in with a uniform solid color (in this example, black). A further examination of the print reveals that only the shadow (dark) areas are recorded.

Interesting and pleasing color may be added to the print by mak-

ing a second negative, with the exposure time reduced by about one-half. This will record the middle tones and add detail to the reproduction.

A third negative may also be made to record the highlights in the photograph, or a screen tint may be made to the size of the reproduction for addition of a third color.

Posterization is a simple and inexpensive procedure for the reproduction of photographs. It does not require the use of contact screens and it provides an excellent opportunity to add color to the reproduction of photographs. We recommend that your first experi-

FIGURE 4–20
Original photograph. (Howard Rose, Jr.)

ence with posterization be limited to reproduction by offset lithography or to a single color in screen printing. Posterization is not practical for relief printing in the graphic arts laboratory.

CONVERTING PHOTOGRAPHS TO LINE DRAWINGS

You can convert a photograph to a line drawing without a high degree of skill, artistic ability, or elaborate equipment. Figure 4–20 shows the original photograph and Figure 4–21 shows how the same photograph looks after it has been converted to a line drawing.

To convert a photograph to a line drawing, attach a piece of transparent acetate over the photograph with tape on all four corners. With a pen and black ink, trace the outline and details of the photograph on the acetate See Figure 4–22.

Most art supply stores stock transparent acetate that has been treated so it will accept black india ink. They also stock a special black ink that will adhere to acetate. It is very important that the acetate and the ink be compatible.

Line drawings made on acetate should be backed with clear white paper when photographed to make negatives. The original drawing on

FIGURE 4–21
Line drawing of photograph in Figure 4–20.

acetate is an excellent transparent positive to make photographic screen printing stencils.

Photographs can also be converted to line drawings photographically. Procedures and equipment are described in *Kodak Tone-Line Process*, Pamphlet No. Q–18, published by Eastman Kodak Co., Rochester, New York.

Duotones

A *duotone* is a two-color halftone print. This process is practical for a beginning graphic arts student in offset lithography.

Two halftone negatives are made of the same photograph. Before exposing the second negative, the contact screen is turned at an angle of 15 to 30 degrees to the first exposure. This prevents a *meshing* of the screens, which would produce an undesirable pattern called a *moiré*. Interesting special effects can be attained when printing a duotone. For example, a snow scene is enhanced by printing the first negative in a light blue and overprinting this with the second negative in black.

FIGURE 4–22
Trace photograph on acetate.

Color Process Printing

Reproduction of color photographs or transparencies requires three- or four-color process printing. This is done by making color separations photographically by using color filters. It requires a separate negative to make plates for each color. A yellow printer, a blue printer, a red printer, and a black printer are usually made. The colors are superimposed over one another on the printed sheet. This is done by making four separate press runs on a single color press. Color reproductions may also be printed on a four-color press, which is actually four printing units one after another. The sheet automatically passes from one printing unit to the next printing unit. Process color printing is beyond the ability and equipment available to most beginners in graphic arts.

Photo Mechanical Transfer (PMT)

Kodak Photomechanical Transfer (PMT) is frequently used as an aid in paste-up copy preparation and for making proofs. It also makes it possible to make positives for photo screen stencils without making negatives.

This process is especially helpful in preparing camera copy when there are several areas in the reproduction job that require different treatment. For example, in the reproduction of a poster, it may be necessary to reduce or enlarge lines of type because the available type for composition is too large or too small. Available illustrations may also require a change in size to be most effective. A photograph may also be a part of the reproduction that requires a reduction or enlargement, making a halftone screen necessary.

By using PMT, each element of a reproduction that requires a different reduction or enlargement, or a combination of line work and halftones, can be reproduced in the form and size required for the reproduction. This makes it possible to assemble a single paste-up for making either a negative or a positive.

It is possible to obtain the same result without using PMT materials, but the procedure is more difficult. For example, it would be necessary to make separate negatives of each element in the image area that required different treatment. A display line may require enlargement to 160 per cent. A paragraph may require a reduction to 80 per cent. An illustration may require a reduction to 60 per cent. A photograph requires a halftone screen. Without PMT, it would be necessary to make separate negatives of each different element. The various negatives would then be assembled on a single masking sheet. This is called *stripping into a flat.*

By using PMT, a positive print is made of each element of copy requiring different treatment. The prints are then assembled in a single paste-up for the camera. A single photographic negative can then be made of the completed paste-up. There are several advantages to using this method. First, it is easier to paste-up positive prints than it is to assemble several negatives on one flat. Second, the paste-up is easier to visualize and change than a series of negatives attached together. Third, old art or type can be converted to clean new art even if the original is yellowed or smudged, thus saving time in retouching negatives. Fourth, minor blemishes on PMT positive prints are easier to correct than on negatives. Fifth, stripping into a flat is easier because you are working with only one negative. Sixth, screen positives can be made directly from the original art work without making negatives.

A complete description of PMT materials and the procedure for their use is described in Kodak Publication No. Q–201.

Proofing Materials

After a paste-up has been made and photographed to make a negative, there is a wide variety of materials available to make a proof prior to making a plate. For black and white proofs, a light-sensitive paper is exposed through the negative, and the paper is usually developed by standard chemistry used to make negatives. 3–M Color Key is a proofing material available in about ten colors and is popular for making color proofs. The *color key sheet* is exposed through the negative. Processing is simple. After exposure, apply color key developer and swab the exposed side of the color key sheet. This removes the unexposed color, leaving the exposed color of the sheet that was selected. These materials and detail procedures for their application are available from Minnesota Mining and Manufacturing Company, St. Paul, Minn.

ACTIVITIES

1. Build Your Vocabulary:
    a. newsprint
    b. ream
    c. caliper
    c. texture
    e. bleed
    f. gripper
    g. register
    h. duotone

2. Design and reproduce a greeting card.
    a. Prepare copy
    b. Make layout
    c. Include either a halftone, line drawing, or screen tint
3. Reproduce examples of screens to make tints available in your laboratory. Include a reverse print and a surprint on each example. On each example print the data on the screen used such as percentage and lines per inch.
4. Conduct an experiment using different colors of paper and different colors of ink.
    a. Cut 100 pieces of paper 3 X 5 in each of four colors: red, blue, yellow, and white.
    b. Print a few words, such as "Color Affects Legibility," on each color of stock on 25 pieces with red ink, 25 pieces with blue ink, 25 pieces with yellow ink, and 25 pieces with black ink.

   c. Prepare charts showing
      1. from highest to lowest legibility,
      2. from most pleasing color combination to least pleasing color combinations.

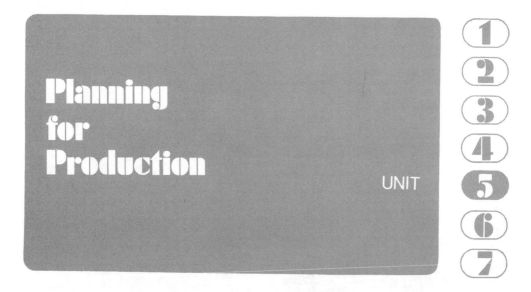

Planning for Production

① ② ③ ④ **⑤** ⑥ ⑦

This unit acquaints you with a logical procedure for planning the reproduction of printed materials.

1. **You will be able to describe a logical procedure to follow for preparing a form for letterpress printing.**

2. **You will be able to plan and prepare camera-ready copy for photographic reproduction.**

3. **You will be able to survey a graphic arts laboratory and list the types of facilities available for reproduction.**

4. **You will be able to select an appropriate printing process for a given job.**

LETTERPRESS

Letterpress is a *relief printing* process. This means the image area is raised above the nonimage area. In order to print the image, all parts must be assembled together, which is called a *form.* All printing surfaces must be type high (0.918 inch) so that when the form is printed each part will receive the same impression.

Words, lines, and paragraphs are assembled in type. Line casting machines, such as the linotype, are used to assemble lines of individual *matrixes,* which are molds of the letters. See Figure 5-1. Each line is then cast with hot metal into a *slug,* which is a type-high metal cast of the characters.

Words and lines can also be assembled by hand, which is called *hand composition.* Each type character is cast on a single body and stored in a type case. The type case has a standard arrangement of small compartments for each letter

FIGURE 5–1
Linotype machine.

and a variety of spaces. Each letter is assembled, one at a time, in a *composing stick.* All lines must be assembled to a uniform length, the stick serving as a guide to attain this. See Figure 5-2. Composition of type cast from metal is commonly referred to as *hot composition.*

Illustrations and photographs are printed with *cuts.* A cut is a metal plate with the image in relief, which is also called a *photo engraving.* A photo engraving is made by transferring the image to a metal plate coated with a light-sensitive acid resist. The plate is developed, removing the acid resist from the nonimage area. It is then placed in an acid bath that eats away the metal in the nonimage area, leaving the image area in relief. Plastic photo engravings are made using the same principle. The engraved plate is mounted on a block of wood or metal to make the cut type high. Cuts are required in the letterpress

FIGURE 5-2
Hand composition. (Saisuki Ieno)

process to print designs, illustrations, and photographs. See Figure 5-3. Most graphic arts laboratories do not have facilities for making photo engravings.

Photo engravings are widely used in industry. It is common practice to make photo engravings of entire pages that might include both type material and illustrations and photographs. This has the advantage of making it practical to compose type by *cold composition.*

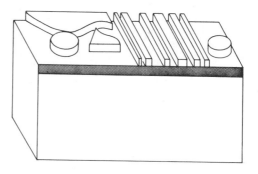

FIGURE 5-3
Typical photoengraving.

Cold composition includes all composition where molten metal is not required. This includes the typewriter, or similar machines such as the VariTyper and all forms of photographic composition. Most laboratories do not use cold composition for letterpress printing.

Because hot metal composition is slow and cumbersome, its use should be limited to the reproduction of a few lines of type. It is practical for printing business cards, tickets, or imprinting a few lines of type in combination with other printing processes. *Reproduction proofs* (proofs to be used in a paste-up for camera-ready copy) are frequently made in graphic arts laboratories when appropriate type styles are available.

Molded rubber relief plates are used in industry for a variety of work but especially for printing corrugated boxes and plastics. *Flexography* is a term used to describe relief printing from rubber plates. With proper facilities, this type of printing would be practical in graphic arts laboratories.

Letterpress Procedures

Like all other printing processes, a plan for the reproduction is essential. This plan is called a *layout.* It might be compared to a blueprint for building a house. Preliminary plans may be in miniature size, but should be in proportion to the finished size. The final layout should always be actual size.

The final layout is used to determine the width of composition, using a *printer's line gauge* which is graduated in *picas.* See Figure 5-4.

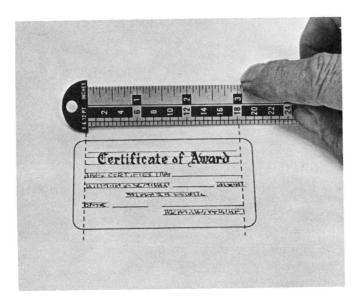

FIGURE 5–4
Determine length of line from layout. (Saisuki Ieno)

The width of composition should be no wider than necessary. Whenever possible avoid fractions of a pica and set all lines in a form the same width.

When the type has been set, transfer it to a *galley* (shallow 3-sided tray), and place the desired space between lines. The thin spacing material used between lines is 2 points thick and is called *leads*; the thicker spaces are 6 points thick and are called *slugs*. Tie up the type form or use *galley locks*.

The next step is to proof the type form. Transfer the type to the proof press and make a print of it. See Figure 5-6.

After the form has been proofed on a sheet of paper, draw lines on the proof to show the finished paper size. This will help you to visualize how the job will look when it is printed. See Figure 5-7. Check the

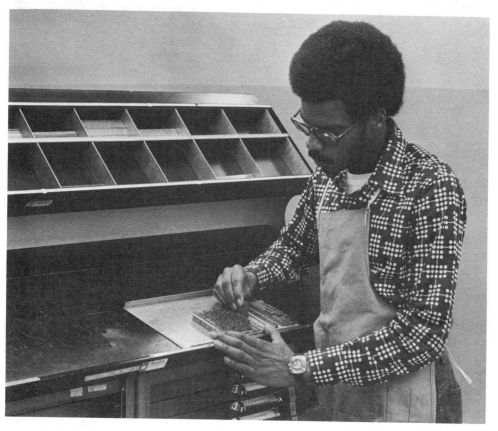

FIGURE 5–5
Space out type on galley.

FIGURE 5–6
Proof type form. (Saisuki Ieno)

proof for typographical errors, spacing between lines, and margin relationships. It may be necessary to make several proof revisions before the form is locked in a chase to be printed on a press. See Figure 5-8.

Other Applications of Letterpresses

Letterpresses are also frequently used for foil stamping, thermography, numbering, scoring, and perforating.

Foil stamping is done by the application of heat and pressure to type or plates in relief. This transfers the foil, which is available in colors as well as in gold and silver, to the material being printed. In graphic arts laboratories, its application is usually limited to hot stamping on book covers or wood products.

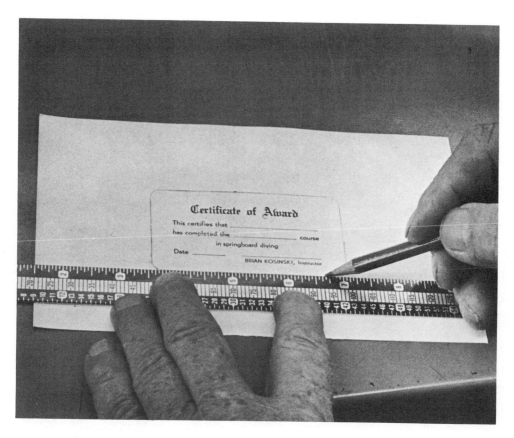

FIGURE 5–7
Draw lines to show paper size. (Saisuki Ieno)

Thermography is an imitation of engraving. Thermography powder is dusted onto wet ink, excess powder is removed, and heat is applied. This results in a raised image. Letterpress is most effective for this process because the ink film is the proper thickness. The film of ink from offset printing is too thin to hold the powder, and in screen printing the ink is too heavy and retains too much powder.

The *numbering* of invoices, purchase orders, tickets, and so on is frequently done by letterpress. Numbering machines in letterpress are made up in the type form as a piece of type or an engraving. With a special relief attachment, it is also possible to number on offset presses.

Scoring means to crush the paper fibers so accurate and smooth folds can easily be made. For short

FIGURE 5–8
Typical letterpress.

runs (about 500 copies) it is recommended that scoring be done on letterpress equipment in school laboratories.

Die cutting is what the name implies. A die is made of a cutting rule, usually type high, which is used to make cut-outs in paper. The box industry uses special die cutting presses. However, successful die cutting can also be done on letterpress equipment in the average school laboratory.

OFFSET LITHOGRAPHY

Offset lithography is a *planographic* printing process. This means that the image area and the nonimage area on the printing plate are on the same plane. In other words, *the printing plate is smooth.*

Alois Senefelder is credited with the development of the lithographic principle in 1798, almost 200 years ago. He found that by writing on limestone with a greasy material he could make reproductions of his writing. The design was first drawn on a flat stone. Next moisture was applied to the entire surface. The surface was then inked with a greasy ink. The moisture repelled the ink in the nonimage area and the grease repelled the moisture in the image area. Therefore ink was retained in the area of the image. When paper was impressed against the stone, a print of the image was made on the paper. By repeating the dampening and inking of the stone, multiple copies could be made. Originally, the term *lithography* meant the art of producing printed matter from stones on which a design had been made. In the fine arts, lithographs from stones are still made today. However, in industry, stones have been replaced with plates made of metal, plastics, and paper. The term *lithography* in industry refers to a planographic type of printing plate and an inking principle based on the fact that grease and water do not mix. In other words, they repel each other. In early days, prints were made directly from plate to paper. However, current practice in industry is to *offset* the design to a rubber blanket. The image is then transferred from the rubber blanket to paper. The term *offset* is generally used to mean offset lithography, and is so used here. In limited applications, relief plates are used to transfer the relief image to a rubber blanket, and from the rubber blanket to the paper.

Preparing Camera-Ready Copy

The procedure and techniques for preparing camera-ready copy is the same for all printing processes. This includes letterpress, offset, and screen printing. The negative (or positive) is made on a reproduction camera designed for this purpose. The negative is used as a mask. When placed over a light-sensitive plate and exposed to a bright light, the emulsion in the image area is hardened. Through development, the emulsion in the nonimage area is washed away. In other words, a photographic transfer of image to a printing plate or stencil requires camera-ready copy. The procedure for making a relief plate, an offset plate, or a screen stencil from a negative (or positive) is different, but the principle is the same.

Prepare Layout

The first step in making a reproduction is to prepare a layout. Figure 5-9 illustrates some typical thumbnail sketches for a poster. They are smaller than actual size, but are in proportion to actual size. Thumbnails are brief sketches that explore different arrangements of the same copy. In other words, they are a method of recording your ideas for further consideration. It might be compared to exploring different roads on a map to arrive at the same place.

FIGURE 5–9
Typical thumbnail sketches of a poster.

Select a thumbnail sketch that you feel is most appropriate for your reproduction. Use this initial visual guide to make a rough layout. Make this layout actual size. Roughly letter the lines of type in the size and style you propose to use. Survey the sizes and styles of type available in your laboratory. Usually it is possible to enlarge or reduce the size of type styles available. However, it is preferable to reduce a large size to a smaller size, rather than enlarge a small size to a larger size. This is because imperfections are reduced in reductions and magnified in enlargements. Do not select a style of type that is not available in your laboratory. Small sizes of type (less than 14 point) are usually indicated with lines, either wavy or straight, to show their length and location. Illustrations or photographs in a rough layout are usually designated by light shaded areas in the appropriate size. In the margin indicate the size and style of type. Figure 5-10 illustrates a rough layout for a poster.

A comprehensive layout is frequently required for many jobs reproduced in industry. A good layout of this kind is almost an exact copy of how the printed piece will appear after it is completed. Skilled graphic artists are employed in industry to make comprehensive layouts so the customer can visualize how the completed job will look. The layout also provides an exact guide for the printer to follow in preparing the composition and

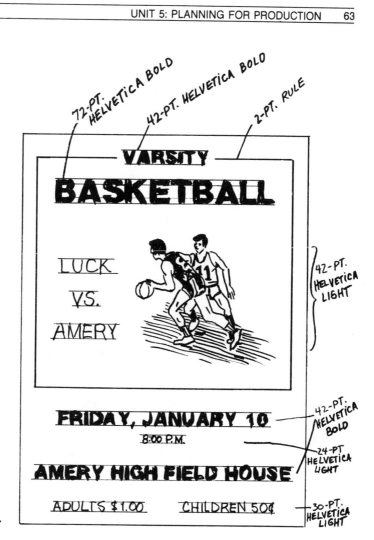

FIGURE 5-10
Rough layout of a poster.

paste-up for the camera. See Figure 5-11.

Comprehensive layouts are desirable, but not always made for every job in schools or industry.

Type Composition

The layouts in Figures 5-10 and 5-11 give specifications for sizes and kinds of type required and their location. This is your guide for composing type.

Type may be composed in hot composition to make repro proofs for your image assembly (paste-up). Composition may also be done on a typewriter. A carbon ribbon is recommended when typing copy to be photographed (Figure 5-12).

The CompuWriter is a photo composing maching (Figure 5-13) which is operated with a keyboard

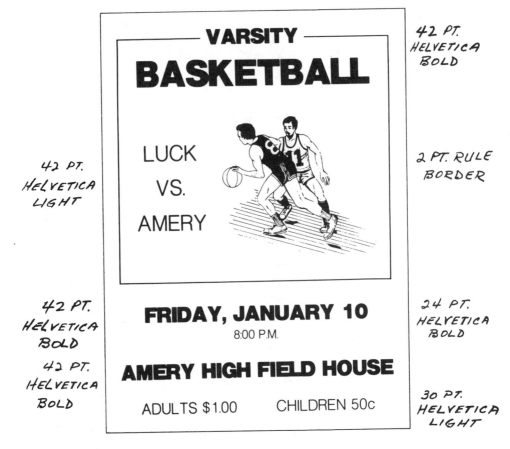

FIGURE 5–11
Comprehensive layout of a poster.

similar to a typewriter. A typist can operate this machine, and others similar to it, after a brief instruction period.

Many other kinds of photo composing machines are available. Some are very simple and inexpensive, while others are more complex and beyond the budget of most graphic arts laboratories. The printout from photo composing machines may be automatically printed and developed, or may require hand processing. Become familiar with facilities available to you and work within these limitations.

Preprinted alphabets are available in a wide variety of sizes and styles of type. Transfer letters consisting of black images on transparent sheets are commonly used. Position the character to be printed in the desired location, then rub the

FIGURE 5–12
Typewriter composition.
(Saisuki Ieno)

FIGURE 5–13
Photo composition. (Saisuki Ieno)

surface of the letter with a blunt instrument. This transfers the letter to the paper. See Figure 5-14. This method of composition is especially useful for a few words or lines of type. These letters will also transfer to transparent acetate. In this case it is also a transparent positive which can be used in making photo screen stencils without making a positive photographically.

Image Assembly

Your final printed job will be no better than your image assembly, or paste-up, as it is frequently called. A layout table or drawing board with "T" square and triangle are helpful for making good paste-ups.

Place a piece of illustration board on your working surface, using the "T" square to square it, and fasten it with masking tape at each corner. A medium weight illustration board with a smooth surface is recommended. A lighter weight material, such as 110 pound index bristol may also be used. The board or bristol should be cut to a size about 4 inches larger on each dimension than the finished size of the printed piece. See Figure 5-15.

Outline the paper size to be printed with black ink in about the center of the illustration board. See Figure 5-16.

Guidelines are used to assist you in properly locating the various parts of the image to be assembled and to keep each part "square"

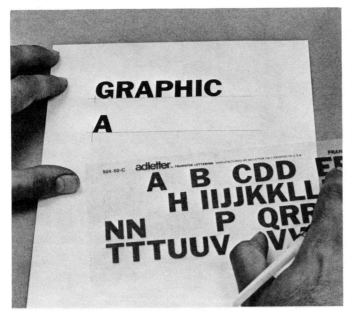

FIGURE 5–14
Transfer letters. (Saisuki Ieno)

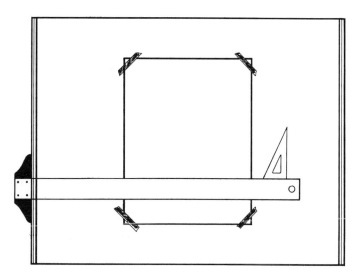

FIGURE 5–15
Attach illustration board on work surface.

with the others. Always make them accurately with a light blue sharp pencil since most photographic film used in graphic arts will not record light blue. Draw lines to indicate the margins for the top, sides, and bottom. See Figure 5-17.

The next step is to draw the guidelines on your board for each part of the image to be assembled. Make horizontal lines for each line or group of lines of type. Make vertical lines to indicate centering, flush left, or flush right. Draw lines

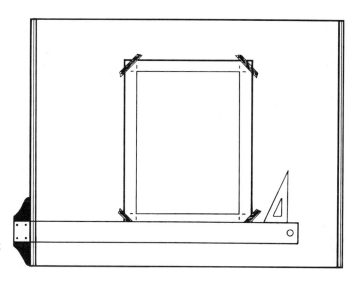

FIGURE 5–16
Outline paper size in black ink.

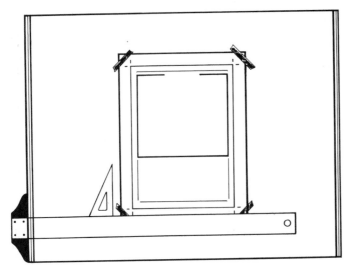

FIGURE 5–17
Draw guidelines for margins.

to show where illustrations are to be located. See Figure 5-18. Your layout is your guide for making the paste-up.

Before proofs or prints of lines of type are trimmed and cut apart for paste-up, draw light blue guidelines under the lines of type that must be cut apart. These lines should extend from the extreme left edge to the extreme right edge of the proof or print. See Figure 5-19. This makes it possible to make a perfect alignment of the proof or print with the guidelines on your board.

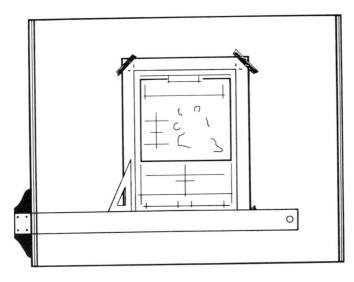

FIGURE 5–18
Draw guidelines for type and illustrations.

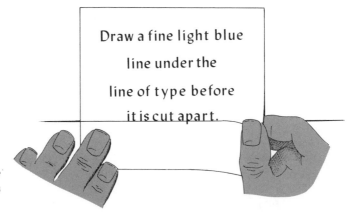

FIGURE 5–19
Draw guidelines under type before cutting lines apart.

There are two common methods of attaching composition and illustrations to the board. These are rubber cement and wax. A special applicator is required for wax. Rubber cement is applied with a brush to the piece being attached to the board. Both materials will permit lifting and relocating a misplaced part on the layout and will not wrinkle the paper. Figure 5-20 shows a completed paste-up.

You will notice that guidelines and the outline of the paper on which the type is printed are visible. Figure 5-21 shows the image of this paste-up as recorded by the camera.

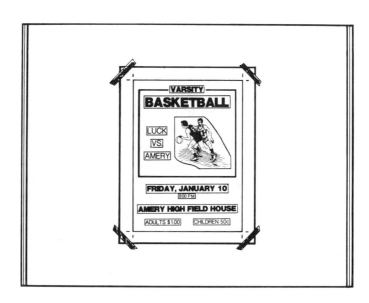

FIGURE 5–20
Paste-up of poster.

FIGURE 5–21
Camera copy of paste-up in
Figure 5–20.

You cannot fool the camera. Dirty specks, smudges, and fingerprints will all create production problems. For this reason, always attach a tissue cover sheet over your paste-up to keep it clean. See Figure 5-22.

The phases of production to follow include camera, stripping, platemaking, stock cutting, and presswork. The procedure in preparation of camera-ready copy is the most difficult for the beginner. It is not only the most difficult, but it also is the most important. Without thoughtful and careful preparation of camera-ready copy, perfect performance in the operations that follow will not be possible and will not result in effective communication or a pleasing reproduction.

The offset process is very versatile. Almost anything that can be photographed can be reproduced in

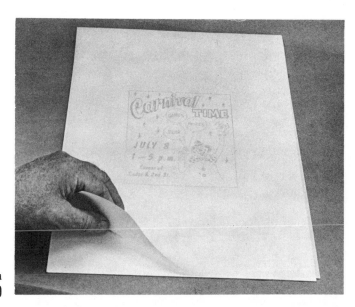

FIGURE 5–22
Protect paste-up with cover sheet. (Saisuki Ieno)

fine detail on rough or smooth paper, from very lightweight paper to thin cardboard. See Figure 5-23.

There are a few disadvantages to offset printing. Small cards, such as business cards, must be printed on larger sheets, then cut apart after printing. A standard postal card is about the minimum size that can be printed. This difficulty can be overcome by running two or three cards on one sheet, then cutting them apart. Negative and plate costs are high on short runs to print a few lines on a sheet. This suggests it would be more practical to print such jobs by letterpress or screen printing if facilities are available.

SCREEN PRINTING

Screen printing is an old art that has developed into an important indus-trial process. Most school laboratories are limited to hand-operated equipment that is simple and inexpensive. See Figure 5-24. The same type of equipment is found in many screen printing plants for short runs. However, in industry automatic equipment is used for specialized work and long runs.

Screen printing is unique because the printing is accomplished by forcing ink through a stencil attached to a screen onto the paper. Silk makes an excellent screen and is the reason this process is frequently called *silk screen* printing. Screens are also made of organdy, nylon, and stainless steel.

Screen printing provides for the heaviest (thickest) deposit of ink of all commercial printing processes. This makes its application most suitable for many kinds of repro-

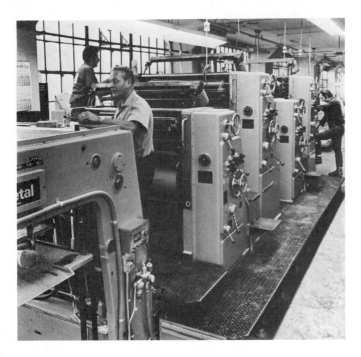

FIGURE 5–23
Offset presswork.

duction where a thick deposit of ink is required.

A further advantage of screen printing is the low cost for making stencils; this is especially important for short runs.

There is practically no limit to size, thickness, or surface that can be reproduced by screen printing. In other words, it is practical to reproduce a small design such as a recipe card, or a street banner 25 feet long.

Stencils may be made in many ways, such as hand cut, tusche and glue, or photographic. For a beginner, the photographic stencil is best because it is simple and does not require a high degree of skill to re-

produce interesting and intricate designs.

Copy preparation, layout, and paste-up for screen printing are the same as for offset reproduction. However, a positive is required instead of a negative to make a photographic stencil. This means that the image to be printed will be opaque, and the nonimage area will be transparent. A transparent positive can be made from a negative by making a contact print on another piece of film. Transparent positives can also be made directly from camera-ready copy by using Kodak High Speed Duplicating film. Excellent transparent positives can also be made from camera-ready copy

FIGURE 5–24
Screen printing is simple.
(Saisuki Ieno)

by using PMT (Kodak's photo mechanical transfer process). See Unit 4.

Designs for positives may also be drawn directly on *Kleer Kote* treated acetate using india ink, or on untreated acetate by using *Artone* acetate ink. Transfer letters may also be attached to the acetate for lettering too difficult to be hand drawn.

Do not overlook the use of designs from nature such as a leaf, dandelion blossom, shaft of wheat, blade of grass, or pressed insect. With a touch of rubber cement, attach to a clear piece of acetate. This will serve as a transparent positive. *Caution:* If the leaf you select is transparent, spray with a fine coat of black lacquer.

Screen printing has many advantages over other printing processes for many kinds of reproductions. It is especially suitable for printing that requires a heavy deposit of ink. A few examples are: printing on textiles, either directly or with transfer paper; printed circuits; decals; reflective signs; posters; and flocking. The heavy deposit of ink makes it practical to print a white design on a black background. The relative cost for short runs is low.

Some disadvantages and limitations of the screen printing process include comparatively low production speed, difficulty of reproducing extremely fine detail, and comparatively slow setting (drying) of the ink.

ACTIVITIES

1. Build Your Vocabulary:
   - a. form
   - b. hand composition
   - c. hot composition
   - d. cold composition
   - e. reproduction proofs
   - f. flexography
   - g. layout
   - h. galley

2. From outside the laboratory, find and bring to class one or more examples of printing. Label the example as to the printing process you think was used to make the reproduction.
3. Make two thumbnail sketches and a rough layout of one job you would like to print in this laboratory. See illustrations in Unit 7 for ideas.

What Can We Print?

UNIT 6

This unit will suggest some meaningful activities appropriate for a beginner in graphic arts.

1. You will be able to identify a meaningful activity that can be reproduced in a graphic arts class.
2. You will be able to identify an approporiate printing process for your reproduction.
3. You will know about jobs that can be reproduced within the limits of your ability, budget, time, and the facilities available in the graphic arts laboratory.
4. You will be able to identify jobs or projects suitable for a cooperative group activity.
5. You will be able to identify jobs for which a manufacturing approach might be most appropriate.

PRACTICAL CONSIDERATIONS

Graphic arts laboratories are not identical. Facilities, budget, space, and instructional time vary. However, interesting, effective, creative, and attractive printed communications can be reproduced in laboratories with limited facilities.

Most of the examples in this unit can be reproduced by more than one printing process. The same job might be reproduced in industry by a different process than the one described here. For example, a recipe card might be reproduced in your laboratory by screen printing; in industry it is more likely to be reproduced by offset. Likewise, a wine label may be reproduced in the laboratory by screen printing the design, and imprinting other data by letterpress; in industry the design is more likely to be reproduced by offset and the personalization may be spotted in by letterpress. In other words, limitations of facilities and number of copies to be printed may mean that it is practical to reproduce a job by one or more processes in the laboratory, but using several processes even though it would not be practical in industry. It is also true that not all shops in industry would use the same printing process to reproduce the same printed item. Experience with each process will provide concepts that will provide a sound basis for understanding the process, its advantages, and its disadvantages.

Examples of possible activities are presented in groups of a similar nature. The activity should be selected on the basis of interest, not on the order presented in this unit. Organization may require grouping people by areas so an entire group does not attempt to work in one area at the same time. Cooperation with your instructor and fellow workers will make your experience most meaningful and rewarding.

GRAPHIC ARTS LABORATORY ACTIVITIES

Recipe Cards

Recipe cards are usually 3 X 5 or 4 X 6. Suitable stock is 90 or 110 pound index bristol. Figure 6–1 suggests a design associated with a kitchen or with cooking. It can be personalized by printing the name of the person who will use the card. In this example, the grain should be in the direction of the long dimension; this makes it easier to type on the card. Recipe cards with a design may be offset or screen printed. Per-

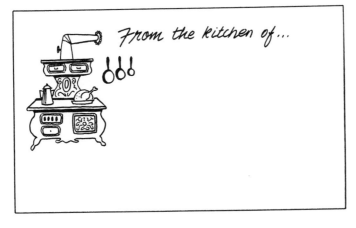

FIGURE 6–1
Recipe card.

sonalized cards without an illustration may be reproduced by letterpress.

Postal Cards

The standard size postal card is 3 1/2 X 5 1/2. Use 110 pound index bristol, or purchase prestamped postal cards sold at all post offices. The "moving" card in Figure 6–2 makes it convenient for families to notify friends of an address change. It is also frequently used in business. Offset is recommended for designs similar to the example. A less intricate design can be screen printed, or a combination of screen printing for the design and letterpress for the wording can be used. Postal cards can also be personalized. Print one or two lines giving the name and address of the sender, leaving as much space as possible for the message.

Personal Stationery

There are two common sizes for personal stationery. Monarch size sheets are 7 1/4 X 10 1/2. Matching Monarch envelopes are 3 7/8 X 7 1/2. This size requires two folds in the sheet to fit into the envelope; the folded sheet is 1/4 inch smaller than the envelope. Note paper is commonly 6 1/2 X 6 3/8. A single fold will fit into a standard No. 6 3/4 envelope, which is 3 5/8 X 6 1/2.

Boxed stationery is available in a variety of sizes; proper size matching envelopes are often packaged with the sheets of paper.

Bond paper substance 20 or text paper, basis weight 60, is most frequently used to print personal stationery. The quality of paper may vary from an inexpensive sulphite bond to more expensive rag content bond. For a first experience, we recommend an inexpensive bond pa-

FIGURE 6–2
Postal card: moving.

per. Text paper with matching envelopes costs about the same as a good quality bond paper and matching envelopes.

Layouts for personal stationery may be formal or informal. See Figures 6–3 and 6–4. As these thumbnail sketches illustrate, the return address information is usually printed on the back flap of the envelope.

Personal stationery provides an excellent opportunity for creative designs. It is not unusual to print the design by offset or screen printing and to imprint the name and address by letterpress. If a background design is printed in the writing area of the sheet, it should be printed by offset in a light color or a very light screen tint. If a screen printed design is used, it should be small and printed in a nonwriting area of the sheet.

Business Stationery

Business stationery includes not only letterheads, shown in Fig-

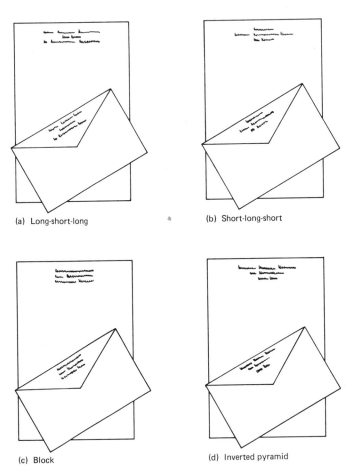

(a) Long-short-long

(b) Short-long-short

(c) Block

(d) Inverted pyramid

FIGURE 6–3
Formal layout for personal stationery.

ure 6–5, but also statements, invoices, and other office forms. Usually the same basic design and color are used on all printed forms of one company. For example, the return address on the envelope might be the same design and color as the letterhead; the size would be reduced in proportion to the smaller area of the envelope. Standard sizes of letterheads are 8 1/2 X 11 (full size), 8 1/2 X 7 1/4 (two-thirds size), or 8 1/2 X 5 1/2 (one-half size). Business stationery is usually printed on substance 20 bond paper. Standard envelope sizes are No. 6 3/4 (3 5/8 X 6 1/2), No. 9 (3 7/8 X 8 7/8), and No. 10 (4 1/8 X 9 1/2). Return address information is usually printed in the upper lefthand corner on the front of the envelope.

Offset reproduction is recommended for examples in Figures 6–5(a), 6–5(c), and 6–5(d). This process would also be appropriate for Figures 6–5(b) and 6–5(e). However, these two examples might also be

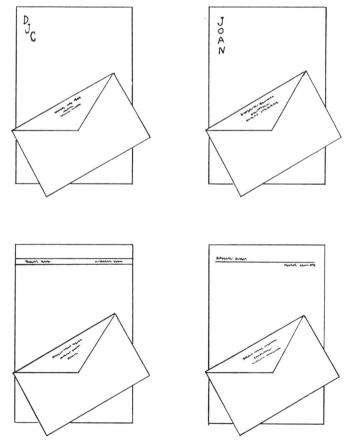

FIGURE 6–4
Informal layout for personal stationery.

Belton Sporting Goods

STERNS DESIGN COMPANY

Centron Art Studio

Neptune Trailers

Jack Peters

FIGURE 6–5
Typical business letterheads.

reproduced by letterpress because there are no illustrations; the composition is limited to a combination of type and rule. Screen printing is seldom used to print business stationery.

Tickets and Cards

Sizes of cards are standard; cards are cut from 22 X 28 bristol, and are packed 500 to a box. The sizes of cards are designated by number: 117, 88, 70, 63, 55, 48, or 36. The number in each case indicates the quantity of cards that may be cut from a full sheet of stock. Size 117 is used for professional cards, but most business cards, tickets, and membership cards are printed in sizes No. 88, 70, or 63.

Typical sizes of cards are as follows:

NUMBER	SIZE
117	1 5/8 X 3
88	2 X 3 1/2
70	2 1/8 X 3 15/16
63	2 5/16 X 3 15/16
55	2 1/2 X 4 3/8
48	2 3/4 X 4 11/16
36	3 X 5 3/16

Elements of card design involve *balance, contrast, emphasis,* and *continuity. Balance* refers to the arrangement of printed matter that will appear in balance to the visual sense. *Contrast* is a variation of spacing or type size or style that relieves monotony and stimulates interest. *Emphasis* is the relative dominance of the printed lines.

Continuity is the harmonious relationships of the various elements. The information should be carefully grouped, spaced, and balanced so it is in a logical order, is easy to read, and eliminates a sense of confusion or crowding.

Since cards are small, you should include only the most important information. For example, in printing a ticket leave out words such as *at, on* and *year.*

Printed cards, as illustrated in Figure 6–6, are small. Letterpress is most suitable for this type of printing because cut cards are too small to print one at a time by offset. Usually the number to be printed is too many to be practical for screen printing. It is possible to print cards by offset if they are *gang printed.* This means printing several cards on one sheet. After printing they are cut apart to their final size. This is common practice in industry by firms that specialize in printing cards. It is also practical in the laboratory. For example, eight workers may wish to print cards. Each worker might prepare camera-ready copy that is then assembled in one paste-up for the camera. One negative, plate, and run would be made. The paper stock would be cut to a size possible to run on the offset press. After printing and drying, the cards would be cut apart.

Certificates

Persons who belong to organizations may be interested in re-

FIGURE 6–6
Typical printed cards.

producing certificates of membership or awards. These are usually printed on a rag content bond or parchment paper substance 24. The recommended size is either 8 X 10 or 10 X 12 so it will fit a standard size frame. See Figure 6–7.

Greeting Cards and Announcements

A wide variety of paper may be used to print greeting cards and an-nouncements. Since most greeting cards have a single fold, making four pages, it is important to select a stock that is opaque enough so you cannot see the printing on the inside page through the cover page. Some recommended papers are basis 70 offset book paper, basis 70 text, and basis 65 cover paper. In making plans for reproducing greeting cards, check on available sizes of envelopes so you can design your card

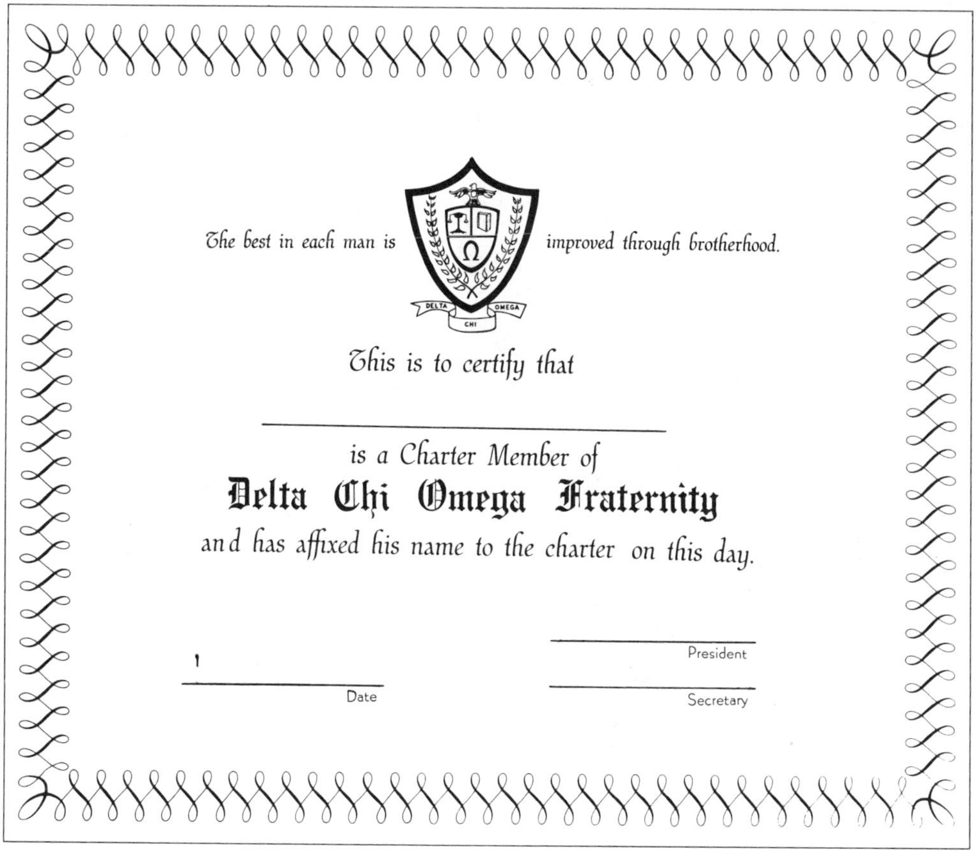

FIGURE 6–7
Certificate.

to fit an envelope. Three common standard sizes are 4 3/8 × 5 5/8, 4 3/4 × 6 1/2, and 5 1/4 × 7 1/4. It is also possible and practical to make a limited number of envelopes, such as 50, by hand. Make plastic *templates* (patterns) to use as guides for cutting and applying glue.

Formal announcements and invitations are frequently printed on vellum stock with matching envelopes. These are usually pur-

FIGURE 6–8
Greeting cards and announcements.

chased in cabinets containing 100 sheets with matching envelopes.

Figures 6–8 and 6–9 show examples of greeting cards and announcements that are not too difficult for beginners to reproduce. The printing process selected is likely to be either screen printing or offset. However, this type of printing can be accomplished with letterpress. Linoleum blocks can be cut for the design and the words composed in type. The process selected should be based upon the na-

FIGURE 6–9
Greeting cards and announcements.

ture of the design. Offset is most appropriate for very fine detail and the reproduction of photographs. Screen printing is suitable for designs with moderate detail. It is not recommended to beginners for reproducing tonal values. Letterpress is ideal for the reproduction of announcements without illustrations. Simple designs with no fine lines or detail may also be reproduced by letterpress. This is done by cutting the design in relief on a linoleum block.

Posters

Most posters printed in graphic arts laboratories are reproduced by either screen printing or offset. The factors determining selection of the printing process include design, size, thickness of stock, and length of run. If the design includes a photograph or a long run (more than 100 copies), offset is indicated. The maximum size as well as the thickness of stock is limited if offset printing is used. It is not practical to print 4-ply poster board on small offset presses. Letterpress is not recommended for poster printing because of design limitations and availability of large sizes of type. Figure 6–10 is an example of a poster design that was especially suitable for screen printing. The number of copies required was less than 100 and they were printed on heavy poster board. Notice how the important information stands out,

such as what, when, where, and why.

PRINTING FOUR PAGES

A greeting card, program, or brochure made of one piece of paper and having a single fold contains four pages. Page 1 is the front; pages 2 and 3 are on the inside when the fold is open; and page 4 is the back page. Remember that a page means one side of a leaf in a book; in other words, each leaf in a book or brochure carries two pages, one on the front and another on the back.

It would be possible to print a four-page brochure by making two press runs. The first form would contain pages 1 and 4, as shown in Figure 6–11, and the second would contain pages 2 and 3, as shown in Figure 6–12. This is called printing *sheetwise.* The *gripper edge* (that is, the lead edge of the paper going into the press) is the same for both runs, while the side guide edge for the second run is on the opposite side of the sheet from the first run.

It is often easier to print four pages at one time in a single press run than to make two runs as when printing sheetwise. The simplest way of doing that is by using a French fold such as is often found on greeting cards. Of course, with this method, one side of the paper remains blank and the leaves are of double thickness. It would not be a

FIGURE 6–10
Screen printed poster.

suitable way of printing a booklet or brochure.

Another way of printing a four-page brochure in a single press run is to cut the paper to a size that is double the finished size. Then, print both sides of the paper with the same form containing all four pages. The last step is to cut the printed sheets into two parts. Each of the double-size press sheets will yield two finished four-page brochures. This procedure can be done in two ways. In one method, called *work* and *tumble,* the sheet is tumbled so the gripper edge for the second run is on the opposite edge of the press sheet from the first run. In the second method, called *work* and *turn,* the sheet is turned over so the same gripper edge is used for both runs, but the side guide edge for the second run is on the opposite side of the press sheet from the first run.

It is always necessary to make a page *dummy* when printing multi-

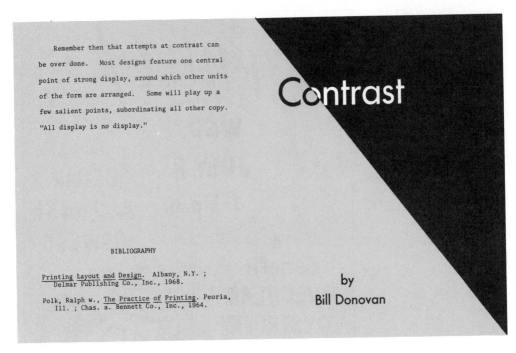

Remember then that attempts at contrast can be over done. Most designs feature one central point of strong display, around which other units of the form are arranged. Some will play up a few salient points, subordinating all other copy. "All display is no display."

Contrast

BIBLIOGRAPHY

Printing Layout and Design. Albany, N.Y. ; Delmar Publishing Co., Inc., 1968.

Polk, Ralph W., The Practice of Printing. Peoria, Ill. ; Chas. A. Bennett Co., Inc., 1964.

by
Bill Donovan

FIGURE 6–11
Sheetwise, printed pages 1 and 4.

ple pages. Cut a piece of paper the size to be printed. For sheetwise printing make a single fold in the sheet and number the pages, indicating the top of the pages with a line.

To make a dummy for printing four pages work and tumble, or work and turn, cut a piece of paper double the finished size. Make a parallel fold and a right-angle fold. See Figure 6–13.

Figures 6–14 through 6–21 show how to number the pages of a 4-page dummy. The tops of all pages should be near the first parallel fold. Indicate the top of each

page by drawing a line. Number righthand pages (odd numbers, 1, 3) in the upper right corner. Number lefthand pages (even numbers, 2, 4) in the upper lefthand corner.

The page dummy shows where each page must be printed in relation to the others so when the job is finished the pages will be in proper position and sequence. This proper positioning of pages is called *imposition.* Note that the sum of the page numbers on pages next to each other on your imposition layout is always one more than the number of pages in the folder. For example, pages 2 and 3 are together and their

CONTRAST

One of the principles of design which finds wide application in putting punch into advertising is that of contrast. Contrast is the use of type, illustrations and other elements of display in such a way to provide the necessary emphasis and variation which imparts life and interest to the page, and gives it an air of attractiveness and appeal. Contrast causes things to stand out and makes them instantly and strikingly apperent. A tall building among low ones or a flash of light at night compels attention by contrast with their surroundings or with what the mind usually associates with normal conditions.

Contrast in typography may be achieved in many different ways, a few of which are indicated in the following examples.

Italic type	*Caution*	do not enter
Bold type	**Caution**	do not enter
Underscoring	<u>Caution</u>	do not enter
Larger size type	Caution	do not enter
Capitals	CAUTION	do not enter
Reverse plate	Caution	do not enter

The examples above make the type talk or, in other words, it makes a person reading it accent certain words. Talking with type is much like speaking before an audience. A speaker that adds force to a few words is much more sucessful than one who shouts out every word. It is the same in display work, as one must avoid the use of too much display lines or groups as well as too many different sizes of type. It is much more effective to accent only one or two words rather than several words.

FIGURE 6–12
Sheetwise, printed pages 2 and 3.

FIGURE 6–13
Make parallel and right-angle fold. (Saisuki Ieno)

FIGURE 6-14
Number page 1 in upper
right corner next to parallel
fold. (Saisuki Ieno)

sum is 5. Recheck your dummy if it does not pass this test.

Use your page dummy to make an accurate layout of the pages to be printed. This should include actual image areas positioned to accurately show margins. See Figure 6-22.

FIGURE 6-15
Open parallel fold to mark
page 2.

FIGURE 6–16
With fold open, mark
page 3.

There are no unbreakable rules that must be followed in determining the size of the image area on a page, or specific space for margins on a page. However, designers agree that the relationship of image area and margins should be an attractive balance. It is desirable that about

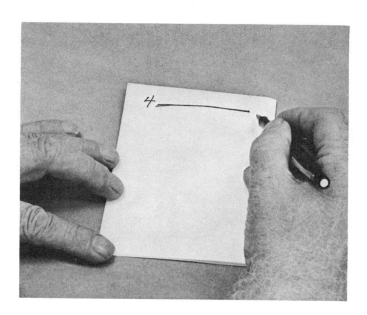

FIGURE 6–17
Close folds, mark page 4.

FIGURE 6–18
Open parallel fold, twist
sheet, mark page 1.

one-half the page area be devoted to the image area and the other one-half to margins.

  There are several formulas for calculating relationships of left, right, and bottom margins. Your authors recommend the following general guidelines. The top margin

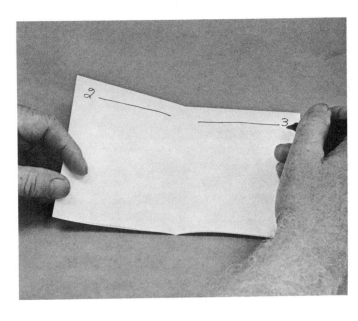

FIGURE 6–19
Close parallel fold, open
right-angle fold, and mark
pages 2 and 3.

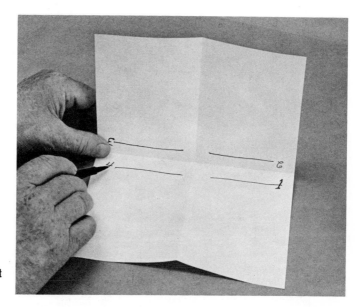

FIGURE 6–20
Open parallel fold, twist sheet, mark page 4.

should be the smallest and the bottom margin should be larger than the top margin. Side margins should be larger than the top margin, but smaller than the bottom margin. Gutter margins (next to the fold), should be slightly smaller than outer margin. See Figure 6–23.

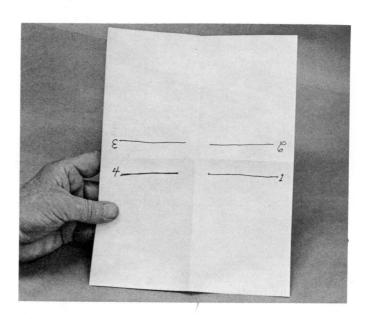

FIGURE 6–21
Complete page dummy.

FIGURE 6–22
Layout showing image area and margins.

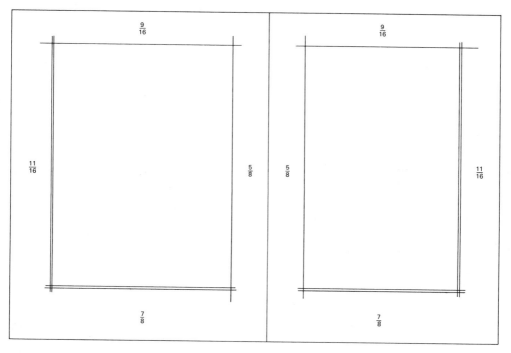

FIGURE 6–23
Pleasing margin relationships.

COPYFITTING

Copyfitting is a procedure for making an estimate of the amount of copy that can be reproduced in a given amount of space. There are two common problems in copyfitting. One problem relates to *display lines.* These are lines of type used for headings in advertisements, posters, programs, letterheads, and so on, which the designer designates as being more important than other parts of the composition. The type size is usually 14 point or larger. The *character count* method of copyfitting is usually employed for estimating the amount of space to be occupied by display lines.

The other problem relates to text or paragraph composition. The designer must estimate the amount of space required to reproduce a given amount of copy. In this case, the *word count* method is usually used.

In other words, the character count method used to fit copy is usually employed for display lines, whereas the word count is usually used to fit copy in larger masses such as paragraphs of text matter.

Character Count

For rough estimates of the amount of space required for a display line, it is common practice to count the letters and spaces in the copy. Each letter or space is counted as one. For example, there are 47 units (characters and spaces) in the following sentence.

Each character or space is counted as one unit.

If the same sentence of copy is reproduced in 18 point Bodoni Bold, count the number of units per pica or per inch from a printed alphabet of 18 point Bodoni Bold that can be fitted into one pica or one inch.

ABCDEFGHIJKLMNO PQRSTUVWXYZ
abcdefghijklmnopqrst uvwxyz

Since the above sentence of copy is predominantly lowercase letters, calculate units per pica or per inch on the basis of the lowercase alphabet in the example above. There are 1 1/2 units per pica or 6 units per inch in the lowercase alphabet. If the sentence had been in all uppercase letters, the uppercase alphabet would have been used to calculate units per pica or per inch.

For more precise estimations using the character count method, thin lowercase letters such as the lowercase *i* are assigned a unit value of 1/2; other lowercase letters such as *n, o, h, e, p* are given a unit value of 1, while larger lowercase letters such as *m* and *w* are assigned a unit value of 1 1/2. Uppercase letters likewise are assigned a unit in proportion to their size. For example, an upper case *H* is given a unit value of 2, an *I* 1, and the *W* or *M* 2 ½.

It should be noted that reference has been made to characters per pica. But characters per inch may also be used to forecast space required for a given line of copy. Both methods are currently used. Layouts made for hot composition are universally made in the printers' system of measure. Lengths of lines and type sizes are designated in picas and points because the composition tools and machines are graduated in this measure. Regardless of the method of composition, the point system is a convenient system of measure because it eliminates the need to work with fractions of an inch. In cold composition by transfer letters, paste-up letters, typewritten composition, and photo composition, more people are making layouts and composing jobs who are most familiar with the more common unit of measure, inches. For all practical purposes, the end result is the same. We recommend using the unit of measure that is appropriate to the method of composition.

Word Count

The space required for paragraphs of text matter should be estimated by the *word count method* of copyfitting. It is used to forecast the amount of space required to reproduce a given amount of copy in a specific size and style of type. It is commonly used because it takes less time to count words than to count characters.

The number of words in a typewritten page is easy to calculate. Count the number of words in 3 lines and divide by 3. This will give the average number of words per line. Count the number of lines on an average page, multiply the average number of words per line by the average number of lines on a page to get the average number of words per page.

Av. no. words per line X av. no. lines per page = average number of words per page.

Find the number of words in a manuscript by multiplying the average number of words per page by the number of pages.

Av. no. words per page X no. pages = words in manuscript.

After the number of words has been determined for a given piece of copy to be reproduced, it is necessary to find out how much space will be required to reproduce the copy. The space required for reproduction depends upon the size and style of type selected and the amount of space between lines.

Estimate the space requirements by first selecting the type size and style desired for the reproduction. For a few paragraphs, the easiest method is to determine how many words set in the selected type can be reproduced in a given length of line. For example, if the length of line is 18 picas (3 inches) and the type selected is 10 point Century School Book, it is necessary to determine how many words can be reproduced in the average 18 pica line. See Figure 6–24.

From Figure 6–24 it is easy to calculate the average number of words that can be reproduced per 18 pica line (3 inches) by counting the number of words in 5 lines 18 picas wide and dividing by 5. In this example, it is 8 words per line.

If the copy contains 80 words and the average number of words per 18 pica line (3 inches) is 8, then 10 lines would be required to reproduce the copy.

The amount of vertical space needed for the copy must also be estimated.

Three lines of 10 point Century School Book (or any 10 point type) would require 30 points (almost ½ inch) of vertical space for reproduction if no space was placed between

Type and its selection in the preparation of material to be presented to the reader is of foremost importance. Designers of type have, over the years, created a vast number of type faces for the printing craft. Years of research

FIGURE 6–24
Find average number of words in 3-inch line.

lines. This is called set *solid,* which means no space between lines. If the lines were leaded 2 points (this means to place 2 points between lines) the 3 lines would require a space of 36 points or ½ inch. In other words, each line of type would require 10 points plus a 2 point lead (space) for a total of 12 points. Twelve points equal one pica. There are 6 picas per inch and therefore the space required for 3 lines would be 36 points or ½ inch.

Most graphic arts laboratories will have type specimen sheets (samples) of type styles and sizes that are available. Figure 6–25 is a typical example of part of a page from a type specimen book from Syracuse Typesetting Company.

Type specimen sheets are an aid in copy fitting and making layouts in a school laboratory. They help not only in making copy fit a limited space, but also make it possible to visualize the end result. It is also desirable to have samples of type for text matter (12 point and smaller) showing the actual size and showing how it appears after it is reduced photographically. See Figure 6–26.

Figures 6–27 and 6–28 show *Compugraphic photo composition* (set by a computer) at 100 per cent, 90 per cent, 80 per cent, and 70 per cent of original size. The first paragraph was set solid (no space between lines); the second praagraph was leaded 1 point (1 point space between lines); and the third paragraph was leaded 2 points (2 points between lines).

Figures 6–27 and 6–28 show that an area required to reproduce a given amount of copy can be adjusted not only by photographic reduction but also by the amount of space between lines. This should be figured out before cold composition of text matter is started. It is not practical to cut apart small lines of type and then paste them together to increase the space between lines. Even for larger sizes of type this should be avoided when possible because of the added time required for image assembly.

Printing Covers

Many varieties of booklet covers may be reproduced in the graphic arts laboratory. Most covers

HAND *Composition* **CORVINUS MEDIUM**

10 POINT▲

TYPE AND ITS SELECTION IN THE PREPARATION OF MATERIAL TO BE
Type and its selection in the preparation of material to be presented to the

12 POINT▲

TYPE AND ITS SELECTION IN THE PREPARATION OF MATER
Type and its selection in the preparation of material to be pres

14 POINT▲

TYPE AND ITS SELECTION IN THE PREPARATION OF
Type and its selection in the preparation of material to

18 POINT▲

TYPE AND ITS SELECTION IN THE PREP
Type and its selection in the preparation o

24 POINT▲

TYPE AND ITS SELECTION IN TH
Type and its selection in the prepar

30 POINT▲

TYPE AND ITS SELECTI
Type and its selection in t

36 POINT▲

TYPE AND ITS SEL
Type and its selectio

FIGURE 6–25
Typical commercial type specimen sheet.

The open spaces between characters or words in lines of print
are created by inserting plain type bodies of varying widths, less
than type high, between regular type characters. The wider ones
are called quads and the others are spaces. Quads and spaces are
not included in fonts of type. Foundry spaces are packaged in job   100%
fonts, but also may be obtained in units or multiples of foundry
lines, explained below. Machine-cast spaces may be found in fonts
or in any quantity from composition houses, where they are cast
on Monotype and other material-makers.

The open spaces between characters or words in lines of print
are created by inserting plain type bodies of varying widths, less
than type high, between regular type characters. The wider ones
are called quads and the others are spaces. Quads and spaces are
not included in fonts of type. Foundry spaces are packaged in job   90%
fonts, but also may be obtained in units or multiples of foundry
lines, explained below. Machine-cast spaces may be found in fonts
or in any quantity from composition houses, where they are cast
on Monotype and other material-makers.

The open spaces between characters or words in lines of print
are created by inserting plain type bodies of varying widths, less
than type high, between regular type characters. The wider ones
are called quads and the others are spaces. Quads and spaces are
not included in fonts of type. Foundry spaces are packaged in job   80%
fonts, but also may be obtained in units or multiples of foundry
lines, explained below. Machine-cast spaces may be found in fonts
or in any quantity from composition houses, where they are cast
on Monotype and other material-makers.

The open spaces between characters or words in lines of print
are created by inserting plain type bodies of varying widths, less
than type high, between regular type characters. The wider ones
are called quads and the others are spaces. Quads and spaces are
not included in fonts of type. Foundry spaces are packaged in job   70%
fonts, but also may be obtained in units or multiples of foundry
lines, explained below. Machine-cast spaces may be found in fonts
or in any quantity from composition houses, where they are cast
on Monotype and other material-makers.

The open spaces between characters or words in lines of print
are created by inserting plain type bodies of varying widths, less
than type high, between regular type characters. The wider ones
are called quads and the others are spaces. Quads and spaces are
not included in fonts of type. Foundry spaces are packaged in job   60%
fonts, but also may be obtained in units or multiples of foundry
lines, explained below. Machine-cast spaces may be found in fonts
or in any quantity from composition houses, where they are cast
on Monotype and other material-makers.

FIGURE 6–26

Typewritten copy reduced. This example of copy was typewritten with pica type (that is, 10
characters per inch), single spaced. For photographic reproduction, it is most desirable to use
a typewriter with a carbon ribbon. A reduction in size will make it possible to fit more copy
into less space. This is often necessary in printing the copy for a program or bulletin.

100%

COMPUWRITER

By adding or reducing space between lines it is possible to make a given amount of copy fit a given amount of space (within limits). You will note that it is easier to read this type when space has been added between lines; however legibility will be reduced if too much space is placed between lines. This size and style of type averages about nine words per line 15 picas in length; in other words 2½ inches in length.

The above paragraph has been set solid

By adding or reducing space between lines it is possible to make a given amount of copy fit a given amount of space (within limits). You will note that it is easier to read this type when space has been added between lines; however legibility will be reduced if too much space is placed between lines. This size and style of type averages about nine words per line 15 picas in length; in other words 2½ inches in length.

The above has been leaded one point

By adding or reducing space between lines it is possible to make a given amount of copy fit a given amount of space (within limits). You will note that it is easier to read this type when space has been added between lines; however legibility will be reduced if too much space is placed between lines. This size and style of type averages about nine words per line 15 picas in length; in other words 2½ inches in length.

The above is two point leaded

90%

COMPUWRITER

By adding or reducing space between lines it is possible to make a given amount of copy fit a given amount of space (within limits). You will note that it is easier to read this type when space has been added between lines; however legibility will be reduced if too much space is placed between lines. This size and style of type averages about nine words per line 15 picas in length; in other words 2½ inches in length.

The above paragraph has been set solid

By adding or reducing space between lines it is possible to make a given amount of copy fit a given amount of space (within limits). You will note that it is easier to read this type when space has been added between lines; however legibility will be reduced if too much space is placed between lines. This size and style of type averages about nine words per line 15 picas in length; in other words 2½ inches in length.

The above has been leaded one point

By adding or reducing space between lines it is possible to make a given amount of copy fit a given amount of space (within limits). You will note that it is easier to read this type when space has been added between lines; however legibility will be reduced if too much space is placed between lines. This size and style of type averages about nine words per line 15 picas in length; in other words 2½ inches in length.

The above is two point leaded

FIGURE 6–27
Compugraphic photo composition 100 per cent and 90 per cent of original size.

are printed on one of three kinds of material. For example, the cover for a Christmas program of 4 pages may be printed on the same material as the inside pages of the program. This is called a *self cover.* The stock may be comparatively light weight, such as 70 pound offset book paper.

For programs, handbooks, or term papers or more than 12 pages, a 65 pound cover stock is recommended. See Figure 6–29. This sam-

80%

COMPUWRITER

By adding or reducing space between lines it is possible to make a given amount of copy fit a given amount of space (within limits). You will note that it is easier to read this type when space has been added between lines; however legibility will be reduced if too much space is placed between lines. This size and style of type averages about nine words per line 15 picas in length; in other words 2½ inches in length.

The above paragraph has been set solid

By adding or reducing space between lines it is possible to make a given amount of copy fit a given amount of space (within limits). You will note that it is easier to read this type when space has been added between lines; however legibility will be reduced if too much space is placed between lines. This size and style of type averages about nine words per line 15 picas in length; in other words 2½ inches in length.

The above has been leaded one point

By adding or reducing space between lines it is possible to make a given amount of copy fit a given amount of space (within limits). You will note that it is easier to read this type when space has been added between lines; however legibility will be reduced if too much space is placed between lines. This size and style of type averages about nine words per line 15 picas in length; in other words 2½ inches in length.

The above is two point leaded

70%

COMPUWRITER

By adding or reducing space between lines it is possible to make a given amount of copy fit a given amount of space (within limits). You will note that it is easier to read this type when space has been added between lines; however legibility will be reduced if too much space is placed between lines. This size and style of type averages about nine words per line 15 picas in length; in other words 2½ inches in length.

The above paragraph has been set solid

By adding or reducing space between lines it is possible to make a given amount of copy fit a given amount of space (within limits). You will note that it is easier to read this type when space has been added between lines; however legibility will be reduced if too much space is placed between lines. This size and style of type averages about nine words per line 15 picas in length; in other words 2½ inches in length.

The above has been leaded one point

By adding or reducing space between lines it is possible to make a given amount of copy fit a given amount of space (within limits). You will note that it is easier to read this type when space has been added between lines; however legibility will be reduced if too much space is placed between lines. This size and style of type averages about nine words per line 15 picas in length; in other words 2½ inches in length.

The above is two point leaded

FIGURE 6–28
Compugraphic photo composition 80 per cent and 70 per cent of original size.

ple also illustrates a *bleed* (printed image that extends to the edge of the sheet) on the top, left side, and bottom. The size of the press sheet is slightly larger than the finished size of the cover.

Extra space around the image provides for at least ¼ inch *gripper* bite at the top of the sheet. Space beyond the image area on each edge provides for rollers to run in a nonimage area to deliver the sheet. Space at the bottom assures that all of the image area will be printed on the sheet. The lines of the inside rectangle indicate where the paper

Trim lines

FIGURE 6–29
Student handbook cover.

will be trimmed after the sheets have been printed. Do not attempt to trim work of this kind until the ink is thoroughly dry. The pressure of the paper cutter clamp will cause one sheet to print on the back of the sheet above if the ink has not set. This is called *set-off* and spoils the appearance of the completed job.

Offset is recommended for printing most self covers, or covers printed on paper cover stock. However, it is also practical to print covers of this kind by screen printing. That process has two limitations: first, the length of run should be 100 copies or less; second, extremely fine detail is difficult to reproduce.

Screen printing or *hot stamping* is recommended for hard covers made with binders board and book cloth. Either process will permit excellent reproduction on a coarse textured material pasted to a heavy board.

Calendars

The printing of calendars provides many opportunities for the practical application of all printing processes. It can also challenge your creative and artistic ability.

This type of activity is suitable for a *manufacturing* approach in the graphic arts laboratory. For example, a group might be organized as a company to design, manufacture, and distribute a product. All factors, from original idea to final sales, might involve each member. It can be equally effective for a cooperative effort of a smaller group. This does not rule out an individual undertaking the reproduction of a calendar, but the complexity of the job must be considered in the light of the time available for its completion.

An example of a seasonal calendar project for a group to reproduce cooperatively is illustrated in Figure 6–30.

Reproduce on a single sheet an appropriate design for each season with a three-month calendar. The theme for fall, representing Sep-

SEPTEMBER						
SUN	MON	TUE	WED	THU	FRI	SAT
1	2	3	4	5	6	7
8	9	10	11	12	13	14
15	16	17	18	19	20	21
22	23	24	25	26	27	28
29	30		FM 1	LQ 9	NM 15	FQ 23

OCTOBER						
SUN	MON	TUE	WED	THU	FRI	SAT
FM 1-30	LQ 8	1	2	3	4	5
6	7	8	9	10	11	12
13	14	15	16	17	18	19
20	21	22	23	24	25	26
27	28	29	30	31	NM 15	FQ 22

NOVEMBER						
SUN	MON	TUE	WED	THU	FRI	SAT
LQ 6	NM 13	FQ 21	FM 29		1	2
3	4	5	6	7	8	9
10	11	12	13	14	15	16
17	18	19	20	21	22	23
24	25	26	27	28	29	30

FIGURE 6–30
Seasonal calendar.

tember, October, and November, might be Halloween, as illustrated. It would be equally appropriate to select a theme of back-to-school, early frost, Thanksgiving, or football, to mention a few possibilities.

For winter, including the months of December, January, and February, there are many possible themes to select. A sampling might include a snow scene, Christmas, Abraham Lincoln, George Washington, basketball, or a valentine.

Spring would include March, April, and May. The illustration might depict a flooded river, early bird catching a worm, cherry blossoms, or baseball.

The three summer months of June, July, and August provide an opportunity for the artistically inclined to make a variety of designs. These might include graduation, boating, camping, swimming, Fourth of July, or vacation.

The same general idea could be expanded to include a single sheet for each month of the year. This would be a more extensive project and would require more time to complete. Likewise, it would be possible to narrow the project down to a single sheet. This might include a photograph as the center of attention with the calendars for the months arranged around the photograph.

Offset is the recommended printing process for calendar reproduction as described here. However, circumstances such as length of run and nature of the design could make calendar reproduction practical for screen printing or letterpress. Reproduction of designs by letterpress would require block cutting in most cases. If linoleum blocks are used for design reproduction, limit the size to a maximum of about 4 X 6 inches. Larger blocks are difficult for the beginner to reproduce.

Basis 70 pound book paper, 65 pound cover paper, 90 pound bristol, or 90 pound index are all suitable for calendar reproduction. These are minimum weights. Slightly heavier paper could also be used.

Labels

Pressure-sensitive paper is recommended for printing labels in the laboratory. This paper is a three-layered sandwich: the face stock (printing surface), the adhesive, and the backing sheet. It is available in a variety of colors and surface finish. All *gum* papers require special handling to prevent curling and difficulties in separating one sheet from another; pressure-sensitive paper is easier to handle than ordinary gummed label paper.

Here are some tips on handling paper for labels. (1) Keep the paper wrapped and stored flat until ready to use. (2) The paper should become accustomed to the temperature and humidity of the laboratory for from two to seven days before it is cut and printed. (3) Cut the paper with a sharp blade and use a light clamp pressure. (4) Cut pressure-sensitive label paper in small amounts (lifts) about 1 inch high or less. (5) If the paper is not printed the same day it is cut, carefully wrap the paper and store flat. (6) If more than one *run* (printing) is to be made on the paper, wrap it between runs. (7) Wipe excessive adhesive from the edges of the pile, and dust with cornstarch or talcum powder. (8) Carefully "fan" the sheets for separation before beginning presswork.

Figure 6–31 illustrates several types of labels that are practical to reproduce in the graphic arts laboratory. Here is an opportunity for several people to work cooperatively in designing and personalizing labels that can be used in the home or a family business.

Individuals might design and reproduce the basic format for different kinds of labels. For example, one person would design and reproduce by offset the *benday* (shading background tint) on the label in Figure 6–32. Enough copies would be printed so that other members of the group could personalize labels for their own use. The name, street address, city, state, and zip code could be imprinted by letterpress. The same procedure could be used for reproduction of bookplates, canning labels, or wine labels. In other words, each member of the group would be responsible for printing a basic design for one label, and would print enough copies to supply other members of the

group. Personalizing the label would be the responsibility of the person who is going to use the label.

Register marks in the upper lefthand and righthand corners in Figure 6–32 are used to aid in the *register* (alignment) of one negative (the benday) with the second negative (the lettering). Assuming both the benday and lettering were printed by offset, two exposures in register would be made on the same plate. The same technique is used to print a job in two colors. Register marks on the art work for each color aid in registering the plate of the first color with the plate for the second color. Note that register marks are located so they will be cut off when the job is trimmed to its finished size.

Decals

The printing of decals requires special decal paper. Simplex paper is recommended. It is coated with a clear water-soluble dextrine adhesive film. This film receives the printed image. When the decal is completed, it is soaked in water and the image on its adhesive film base is slid off onto either an opaque or transparent surface. If the decal is to be used on the inside of a transparent surface, such as a car window, the image must be printed in a wrong-reading position.

Printed Circuits

Screen printing is widely used to print the electrical conductors

FIGURE 6–31
Typical printed labels.

used in electrical circuits. The components are attached to the circuit board after the board has been printed and etched.

There are several types of material used to make circuit (wiring) boards. G-10 glass epoxy board that has a copper surface on a transpar-

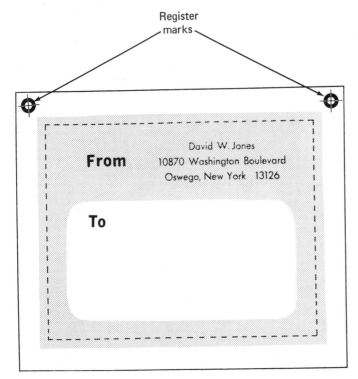

Register
marks

From

David W. Jones
10870 Washington Boulevard
Oswego, New York 13126

To

FIGURE 6–32
Parcel post label.

ent base is recommended for graphic arts laboratories.

The *first step* is to design the circuit and make a drawing with black ink on white paper. See Figure 6–33.

The *second step* is to make the photographic stencil and adhere it to the screen. Prepare for printing in the usual way.

The *third step* is printing. Instead of using ink, print the design on the copper surface of the wiring board with an acid resist.

The *fourth step* is to etch the board after the resist is completely dry. Be especially careful to avoid scratching the printed design. Ferric chloride is a suitable etchant (etching solution). Place this in a shallow tray, deep enough to cover the board and slightly larger than the board. Place the printed side of the board toward the bottom of the tray. Light shaking will produce a more even distribution of the etchant; it also reduces the etching time, which might vary from 5 to 15 minutes depending upon strength and temperature of the etchant. Etching is complete when the copper in the nonimage area has been eaten completely away by the etchant.

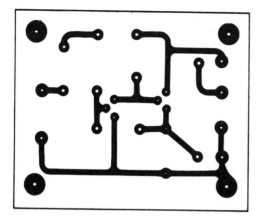

FIGURE 6–33
Drawing ready for camera.

6–34. *First,* the image can be printed directly on textile material. Use an ink designed for textile printing and be sure to follow the directions provided by the manufacturer. *Second,* the image can be printed on transfer release paper. The design is then transferred to the textile material with heat and pressure. An ordinary iron may be used.

Transfer release paper for printing on textiles is recommended for the beginner. The procedure is the

The *fifth and last step* is to clean the board. Wash thoroughly under running water to remove all traces of etchant. Remove the acid resist from the surface of the circuit with a solvent.

Caution: Ferric chloride and other acids that might be used for etching circuit boards are caustic; they will burn your skin and produce fumes that are harmful to breathe. In handling this material, wear safety glasses, a rubber apron, and rubber gloves. In mixing acid solutions, always add the acid to water. Do not pour water into acid. Work in a well-ventilated area, and do not inhale fumes of the etching solution.

Printing Textiles

Screen printing of textiles can be done by two methods. See Figure

FIGURE 6–34
Screen printed "T" shirt.

same as for screen printing other materials with two exceptions. (1) Use a special ink recommended for the transfer release paper. Ordinary poster inks will not work. (2) In making the photographic screen stencil, the transparent positive must be placed over the photo stencil material in reverse of normal procedure. In other words, the positive will be *right reading* when placed in the exposure frame.

ACTIVITIES

1. Build Your Vocabulary:
    a. balance
    b. contrast
    c. emphasis
    d. continuity
    e. gang printed
    f. printing sheetwise
    g. work and tumble
    h. work and turn

2. Select, design, and reproduce a product using letterpress.
3. Select, design, and reproduce a product using offset.
4. Select, design, and reproduce a product using screen printing.

After the Job is Printed

This unit explains common finishing operations essential to successful completion of printed communications.

1. You will be able to plan an effective inspection procedure.
2. You will be able to identify appropriate finishing operations for different types of jobs.
3. You will be able to outline steps required to complete a job after it has been printed.

FINISHING OPERATIONS

Inspection

All work should be inspected for imperfections after the ink is dry. Drying usually takes several hours. Printing done on one day should not be inspected until the next day. Printed material is easily soiled and for this reason the work surface and the hands of the inspector must be clean. The first inspection should be done before the job is cut apart, trimmed, folded, or fastened together in any way.

Jog the pile of paper to align the edges of the stock. Be careful to keep all sheets with the heading in the same position. Leaf through the entire pile, inspecting the printing on both sides of the sheet.

After the first inspection, you should continuously watch for defective sheets as the paper is being handled in the finishing operations.

The final inspection should be done just before packaging.

Padding

Padding is the application of a flexible adhesive to one edge of the pile to hold the sheets together. Always allow ⅛ to ¼ inch for trim on each of the three other edges after the paper has been padded.

Cutting Apart and Trimming

Double check the paper cutter setting before cutting jobs apart or trimming. A mistake at this point can spoil the whole job. Keep track of edges as they are trimmed to avoid a double trim on one edge.

Pamphlet Binding

Pamphlets of more than four pages should be assembled after folding. This operation is called *gathering* or *collating.*

Prior to *stitching* (stapling), the assembled pamphlets should be inspected again. It is easier to correct errors such as removal of double sheets before the pamphlet is fastened together.

If the pamphlet contains more than 12 pages, three edges should be trimmed. A trim allowance of from ⅛ to ¼ inch should be provided for on the top, fore-edge, and bottom.

Bookbinding

Books are commonly bound by one of three methods: (1) *edition binding,* (2) *perfect binding,* or (3) *mechanical binding.*

Textbooks are good examples of *edition binding.* Printed sheets of paper are folded into sections of 16 or 32 pages, called *signatures.* These sections are assembled and sewn together by special sewing machines. Covers (cases) are made to fit the book. These are made of binder's board covered with book cloth. Edition binding can be done by hand in your laboratory with fairly simple equipment.

Perfect binding is widely used for paperback books. Most telephone books and similar books are *perfect* bound. After the signatures have been collated, the backs are ground off leaving a rough surface. A special adhesive is applied, and the cover is glued into place. The books are then trimmed on three edges. Most graphic arts laboratories are not equipped to do perfect binding.

Mechanical binding refers to plastic and wire binding frequently used for school notebooks and other books which must open flat. A series of round or slotted holes are punched along the binding edge. The binding material is then inserted into the holes. Allowance must be made for the type of mechanical binding being used. In designing books for this type of binding, it is also necessary to plan for ⅛ to ¼ inch trim at the top, fore-edge, and bottom. Books should be trimmed *before* holes are punched.

Final Inspection

All printed material should be given a final inspection before packaging.

Packaging

Neatly wrap and clearly label all printed material. The first impression the user of printed material receives is from the appearance of the package. A neat package immediately communicates to the user that the contents in the package were carefully and neatly done.

ACTIVITIES

1. Build Your Vocabulary:
    - a. padding
    - b. collating
    - c. edition binding
    - d. perfect binding
    - e. mechanical binding
2. Outline an inspection procedure for a specific job to be reproduced.
3. List two examples of printed jobs that require an allowance for trim in designing a job to be printed.
4. Describe one example where space allowance must be made on the binding edge of a printed job.

REFERENCES

Biegeleisen, J. I., *Silk Screen Printing Production.* New York: Dover Publications, Inc., 1963.

Carlsen, Darvey E., *Graphic Arts.* Peoria, Ill.: Chas. A. Bennett Co., Inc., 1970.

Cogoli, John E., *Photo-Offset Fundamentals.* Bloomington, Ill.: McKnight and McKnight Pub. Co., 1973.

Eastman Kodak Company, *Kodak Graphic Arts Handbook.* Rochester, N.Y.,

Felten, Charles J., *Layout, Printing Design & Typography.* St. Petersburg, Fla.: Charles J. Felten, 1971.

Flexographic Technical Association, *Flexography: Principles and Practices,* Flexographic Technical Association, 1962.

Koslof, Albert, *Screen Process Printing.* Cincinnati, Ohio: Signs of the Times Pub. Co., 1964.

Perry, Kenneth F., *The Binding of Books.* Bloomington, Ill.: McKnight and McKnight, 1967.

Polk, Ralph W., *The Practice of Printing.* Peoria, Ill.: Chas. A. Bennett Co., Inc., 1964.

Silver, Gerald A., *Modern Graphic Arts Paste-Up.* Chicago: American Technical Society, 1973.

Stevenson, George A., *Graphic Arts Encyclopedia.* New York: McGraw Hill Book Co., 1968.

Turnbull, Arthur T. and Russell N. Baird, *The Graphics of Communication.* New York: Holt, Rinehart and Winston, Inc., 1968.

Updike, Daniel Berkley, *Printing Types: Their History, Forms and Use,* Vols. I and II. Cambridge, Mass.: Harvard University Press, 1962.

Index